SIGNS &
WONDERS
AND
EVANGELICALS

SIGNS & WONDERS AND EVANGELICALS

A Response to the Teaching of John Wimber

Robert Doyle, General Editor

SIGNS & WONDERS AND EVANGELICALS
Copyright © 1987 by Robert Doyle

LANCER Books
3-5 Richmond Road
Homebush West, NSW 2140
Australia

All rights reserved. No portion of this publication may be reproduced in any form or by any means without the prior written permission of the publisher.

ISBN 0-85892-367-X

7898 RBP 987654321

Printed in Australia by
Robert Burton Printers Pty Limited
63 Carlingford Street, Sefton, N.S.W.

TABLE OF CONTENTS

Preface ... 1

Part One: Signs & Wonders and Evangelical Ministry
John Woodhouse

1. A Call to Renewal ... 7
2. John Wimber on Signs and Wonders ... 13
3. Signs and Wonders in the Bible ... 17
4. Signs and Wonders and Evangelical Ministry ... 37
5. The Miraculous and the Christian Life ... 45
6. Conclusion: Two Ways to Leave ... 57
   Addendum - Methods of Argument ... 59

Part Two: Paul, the Miraculous and Ministry
Paul Barnett

7. The Challenge to Paul's Ministry ... 73
8. 2 Corinthians ... 79
9. Miracles and Ministry Today ... 95

Part Three: Historical Perspective
John Reid

10. The Great Evangelical Awakening 101

Conclusion: Thinking through the Implications
Robert Doyle

11. Our Experience of God 117

End Notes 125

PREFACE

This book has its beginnings in pastoral concern expressed by the committee of the Evangelical Fellowship in the Anglican Communion (EFAC), Sydney—a concern raised by the recent visit to Australia of John Wimber. John Woodhouse is head of the Department of Old Testament at Moore Theological College, Paul Barnett is a lecturer in New Testament and Master of Robert Menzies College at Macquarie University, John Reid is Bishop of South Sydney, and Robert Doyle is a lecturer in Church History and Systematic Theology at Moore Theological College. All four have regular preaching and pastoral responsibilities in Sydney churches.

John Wimber, successful pastor of one of the largest and rapidly growing churches in southern California, and author of two books on the subject of 'signs and wonders', has a compelling message: Christians must seek, and boldly use miracles in public worship and preaching.

Wimber's appeal is wider than southern California and his two books, *Power Evangelism* (1985) and *Power Healing* (1987), for he has a sizeable convention ministry in the English-speaking world and the mainline churches. He was long an associate and friend of David Watson. Psychiatrist and popular Christian writer John White is appreciative of John Wimber's ministry. Most who have attended his conferences or engaged in in personal conversation describe him as a warm and genuine person.

John Wimber's call to 'power evangelism', by bringing 'spiritual gifts' out of the closet of private practice into public ministry, is being taken very seriously. Wherever he has conducted conventions—in the United States, Canada, the United Kingdom and New Zealand—many evangelical Christians have been captivated, motivated and become committed to his call to a radical re-evaluation of our church activities.

Through relating his own experiences, and interpreting the ministry of Jesus and the apostles, Wimber argues that the presence of eye-catching, supernatural phenomena is properly a normal part of Christian activity. Its absence is serious, and weakens effective evangelism. In his books and on the convention platform John Wimber argues this case, and shows how to recapture the power and wonder of the apostolic age.

Following the announcement of his Australian visit, and in light of *Power Evangelism* and *Power Healing* and news of earlier conventions, the Sydney committee of EFAC raised the question of what pastoral guidance might we offer our members, and evangelicals in general. We started by circulating amongst ourselves biblical, theological and historical papers on Mr Wimber's claims and the Bible's own teaching on 'signs and wonders'. Two preliminary studies were published in the diocesan magazine *Southern Cross*, and then the three papers which make up the bulk of this book were presented at a specially convened conference.

It is a mark of a widely felt concern that a weekday-morning conference called at short notice attracted over 150 ministers from various denominations.

That concern is the subject of this book.

It is primarily over the Bible. Is what John Wimber says true to the teaching of the Bible? What *does* the Bible teach about 'signs and wonders' and effective gospel ministry? For even if Mr Wimber's claims are in the end found to be seriously deficient, he has acutely raised important issues that demand answers and call for decisions. These issues are so crucial, and Wimber's persuasiveness so keenly felt, that the response may affect the shape of Christian ministry for a long time to come.

Although John Wimber is the subject of this book, the main focus is what St Paul's message terms 'the ministry of reconciliation, that God was reconciling the world to himself in Christ'. The activity of God in the cross—the activity of God in the world—is our major theme.

We express our gratitude to Margaret Kirton for her careful work in preparing the manuscript.

Robert Doyle
1 December 1987

Part One

SIGNS & WONDERS AND EVANGELICAL MINISTRY

by

John Woodhouse

Chapter One

A CALL TO RENEWAL

Christianity is supernatural. Being a Christian is a supernatural matter. When Christianity is reduced to either formal ceremonies or to theological ideas it is no longer authentic. New Testament Christianity is not a matter of the mind only, any more than it is a matter of mere formality.

Many who are involved in evangelical ministry today recognise that we evangelicals have at times forgotten this. Our churches—or some of them—have become places of formal religion for those who like that sort of thing, or places of learning only, where knowledge increases, but there is no trembling at God's word (see Isa 66:2). And many Christians are tired of their 'religion,' fearing that they have 'a form of religion while denying its power' (2 Tim 3:5).

If all this is correct, it is time for repentance. It is time to humbly hear the warnings of the New Testament: 'Let anyone who thinks that he stands take heed lest he fall' (1 Cor 10:12). 'How much more severely do you think a man deserves to be punished who has trampled the Son of God under foot, who has treated as an unholy thing the blood of the covenant that sanctified him, and who has insulted the Spirit of grace?' (Heb 10:29, NIV) It is time to renew our faith in God, and to set about living that faith.

John Wimber seems to be calling us to just such a renewal. His books, tapes and conferences are reaching large numbers of evangelical Christians who sense the problem that I have described. The unmistakable call from John Wimber is to a Christian life which is open to the direction of God moment by moment, which does not presume to know in advance what God is going to do, but which believes that he is active in the world today just as he was active in the days of the New Testament. This is certainly not a religion of the mind only. It is a religion of power, where the supernatural activity of God is expected day by day, particularly in 'words of knowledge,' miraculous healings and the driving out of demons.

I believe that much of John Wimber's appeal lies in the relevance of the diagnosis: Evangelical Christianity today *is* often a weak caricature of what it ought to be. But I believe that John Wimber's prescription, while attractive in many ways, is wrong. Two illustrations will begin to suggest what I mean.

As far as I can remember in my Christian life, I have always believed in praying for the sick—for their healing. I believe that God answers prayer, sometimes in ways that we judge remarkable, sometimes in ways that we are foolish enough to take for granted. And I do not only believe it, I do it. And I am thankful to God that I have seen what I think of as remarkable answers to my prayers. I confess that I pray for the sick most consistently when the sick is me. I actually don't know any

Evangelical Ministry

Christian who does not believe in and practise prayer for the sick when they are the sick! That, of course, is not any more adequate than praying for the government only when war breaks out.

So it is good to be called on to pray, to look to our heavenly Father for all our needs, and to trust him. It is especially good for those of us who have become slack at praying to be told that true Christians believe that God is both their Father and the sovereign Lord of all things. True Christians must be people who pray. I am for praying, and I am for doing it more, and that includes praying for the sick.

But I do not believe that prayer for the sick is a special category of prayer which requires a special theology, and special instruction. Prayer is primarily, in the Bible, Petition addressed to God. Healing is one thing among many for which we may pray. When I pray for someone who is sick, this is not something that is in principle different from my prayers for the government, for drought relief, for safety on the roads or for my daily bread. And healing is not the only or necessarily the most important thing to pray for the sick. Furthermore, it is no greater miracle if God restores someone to physical health than if his Spirit produces the fruit of love, joy, peace, patience, kindness, goodness, faithfulness, gentleness and self-control (Gal 5:22-23), *despite continued sickness*. That is a God-glorifying work of the Holy Spirit.

John Wimber is right, then, about Christians needing to be people who pray, but he is wrong to place such importance on one kind of prayer and one kind of answer (namely, healing), for then the less spectacular (what Wimber calls 'natural'!) works of God's Spirit are undervalued.

Secondly, I am for greater faith in the power of God. I speak for myself: There is a great deal of room for growth in such faith. I am still anxious about many things very often. The promise of Jesus, 'Seek first the kingdom of God and his righteousness and all these things will be given to you as well' (Matt 6:33), does not shape my life and my decisions as clearly as it should. Why? Because my faith in the power of God is weak.

So it is good to be called on to believe more confidently and consistently in God's power, and to do so in practice. But I do *not* believe that contemporary 'signs and wonders' are the display of the power of God which I should seek.

All this means that, as I have read the writings of John Wimber[1] and listened to him speak, I recognise and (for my own part) acknowledge many of the deficiencies he sees in much evangelical Christianity. But as I listen to his proposed solutions and his understanding of what the Christian life ought to be like, I find myself more and more disturbed. My purpose in the pages that follow is to explain why.

In chapter 2 I will briefly outline John Wimber's teaching about 'signs and wonders' today.

The question that then arises is: Are these 'signs and wonders' the same as what the Bible calls 'signs and wonders'? Do they—as John Wimber

Evangelical Ministry

teaches—belong to the same category? Do they have the same purpose and function? A third chapter, therefore, will survey what the Bible calls 'signs and wonders' and their role in the purposes of God for his people so that we can address these questions.

In a fourth chapter we will explore the consequences of Wimber's theology of 'signs and wonders'. Is this still evangelical Christianity?

Finally, I will attempt to provide a biblical perspective on what Wimber calls 'signs and wonders'.

An appendix will analyse the kinds of argument which enable John Wimber to come to such different conclusions from this writer, using the same Scriptures.[2]

In all this I hope that we will not lose sight of the fact that criticism of John Wimber's teachings is not meant to be a defence of the status quo. I hope that those who find themselves in general agreement with what I have written will at the same time be renewed in their commitment to,

> be strong in the Lord and in the strength of his might. Put on the whole armour of God, that you may be able to stand against the wiles of the devil . . . Stand, therefore, having girded your loins with *truth,* and having put on the breastplate of *righteousness,* and having shod your feet with the equipment of *the gospel*

of peace; above all taking the shield of *faith,* with which you can quench all the flaming darts of the evil one. And take the helmet of *salvation,* and the sword of the Spirit, which is *the word of God* (Eph 6:10-17).

Chapter Two

JOHN WIMBER ON SIGNS AND WONDERS

The main elements in John Wimber's message and theology, as I understand them, are as follows.

Signs and wonders and the kingdom of God

The central idea is the kingdom of God,[3] inaugurated at the first coming of Jesus, and to be consummated at his return. Since the kingdom has come and is a reality, but has not yet fully come, the present time is a time of war and conflict between the kingdom of God and the kingdom of Satan. The most important thing for those who enter the kingdom of God, therefore, is to correctly understand power and authority in this conflict.

> We [Christians] are thrust into the middle of a battle with Satan, a tug-of-war—the prize being the souls of men and women. Satan's captivity of men and women has many facets, denial of final salvation being his primary goal. But there are other types of dominion: bondage to sin, physical and emotional problems, social disruption, demonic affliction. Our mission is to rescue those who

have been taken captive as a result of Adam's fall.[4]

How do we engage in this battle? What are our weapons? Our weapons are the power of the Holy Spirit manifested in the gifts of the Spirit. *We engage in the battle by doing what God tells us, not just through the Scriptures, but through learning to hear his voice anywhere and everywhere.*[5]

The individual occasions when the kingdom of God and the kingdom of Satan clash are called by Wimber 'power encounters'.[6]

> A power encounter is a visible practical demonstration that Jesus Christ is more powerful than the false gods or spirits worshipped or feared by a people or group.[7]

Power encounters, in Wimber's understanding, involve such events as casting out demons, healing the sick, and 'words of knowledge' (defined as 'God revealing facts about a situation concerning which a person had no previous knowledge'[8]). Such 'signs and wonders' are therefore necessary manifestations of the kingdom of God in the present age. They are the weapons by which the war is waged.

Signs and wonders and evangelism
It follows that such 'signs and wonders' will have an important role in evangelism. After all, when is

Satan's kingdom most under attack if it isn't when the gospel is being proclaimed! Wimber calls evangelism with signs and wonders 'power evangelism'. He says,

> In power evangelism, resistance to the gospel is overcome by the demonstration of God's power in supernatural events, and receptivity to Christ's claims is usually very high.[9]

Power evangelism is different from traditional evangelism, which Wimber calls 'programmatic evangelism'.[10] He argues that in traditional message-centred, rationally presented evangelism with some appeal to the emotions, people may make decisions for Christ, but many such people 'do not encounter God's power, and thus do not move on to a mature faith. Because there is something inadequate about their conversion experience, later growth for many is retarded'.[11] The argument is not that traditional evangelistic methods have all been wrong, but that they have often been 'incomplete, lacking demonstration of the kingdom of God in signs and wonders'.[12]

Signs and wonders and faith

Wimber's call, therefore, is not simply that Christians should realise that God is great and can heal the sick. He is saying that faith in God, if it is going to be mature and strong, must see or 'encounter' God as great and the healer of the sick. Words are not enough. He says,

> . . . power encounters authenticate conversion experiences in a way that mere intellectual assent does not. This gives new Christians confidence about their conversion, a solid foundation for the rest of their lives.[13]

Signs and wonders, then, confirm and assure the Christian's faith. It is no accident, therefore, that the healings and expulsions of demons and words of knowledge are not just called 'miracles' in Wimber's theology, but 'signs and wonders'. This is a biblical expression carrying very significant connotations, which I will outline in the next chapter.

Chapter Three

SIGNS AND WONDERS IN THE BIBLE

This is not going to be a study of the miraculous in the Bible. It is in some ways narrower than that, and in some ways broader: Not all miracles are 'signs and wonders', and not all 'signs and wonders' are miracles. The questions I want to ask are: What does the Bible call 'signs and wonders'? What is the place of 'signs and wonders' in Bible-based Christianity?

These questions are very important if we are going to assess John Wimber's message from the Bible. The most important question is not whether 'miracles' are occurring at the hands of John Wimber and others, but what *place* these phenomena have in their understanding and living. After all, as we shall see, even the antichrist is expected to perform wonders! The *place* that these things have in Wimber's theology is summed up by the biblical label he gives them, 'signs and wonders'.

The expression 'sign and wonder'[14] describes an event which causes wonder, and which is significant. 'Wonder' suggests the nature of the event. 'Sign' suggests its function. It is a 'wonderful sign', or a 'significant wonder'.

It is important to realise that the Bible uses this expression in a limited way. Only a small number of very particular events are described as 'signs and wonders'.

Signs and wonders and our redemption

The first and most obvious events which the Bible calls 'signs and wonders' accompany the historical redemptive acts of God.

In the Old Testament, the deliverance from Egypt and the bringing of Israel to the promised land was by means of God's 'signs and wonders'. Before the event God said,

> . . . I will multiply my *signs and wonders* in the land of Egypt . . . (Ex 7:3).[15]

After it Moses said,

> Has any god ever attempted to go and take a nation for himself from the midst of another nation, by trials, *by signs, by wonders,* and by war, by a mighty hand and an outstretched arm, and by great terrors, according to all the Lord your God did for you in Egypt before your eyes? (Deut 4:34).[16]

All future generations of Israelites were to remember and say,

> . . . the Lord brought us out of Egypt with a mighty hand and an outstretched arm, with great terror,

> with *signs and wonders* . . . (Deut 26:8).[17]

And some of them did remember:

> He it was who smote the first-born of Egypt,
>   both of man and of beast;
> who in thy midst, O Egypt,
>   sent *signs and wonders* against Pharaoh and all
>   his servants (Ps 135:8-9).[18]

From the New Testament perspective Stephen recalled the exodus events in these terms:

> God . . . led them out, having performed *wonders and signs* in Egypt and at the Red Sea, and in the wilderness for forty years (Acts 7:36).

If you ask what are the 'signs and wonders' of which the Old Testament speaks, the first answer is that they are the events by which God redeemed his people from Egypt and brought them to the promised land. They are the judgments God inflicted on Egypt which led to the deliverance of his people.

Are any other events called 'signs and wonders' in the Old Testament? At this point we should notice two other categories of 'signs and wonders'.

They are variations of the 'signs and wonders' we have just seen.

Firstly, the curses that will fall on the people of Israel if they fail to keep the covenant are described as follows:

> All these curses shall come upon you and pursue you and overtake you, till you are destroyed, because you did not obey the voice of the Lord your God, to keep his commandments and his statutes which he commanded you. They shall be upon you as *a sign and a wonder,* and upon your descendants forever (Deut 28:45-46).

In other words, the signs and wonders that God did against the Egyptians, which effected the redemption of Israel, will be done against Israel if Israel will not obey. The expression 'a sign and a wonder' here underlines the fact that this judgment will be a reversal of the blessing of redemption.[19]

Secondly, towards the end of the Old Testament period, when the nation of Israel had fallen under God's judgment, we read in the book of Daniel of two occasions when God delivered his faithful servants from the power of the pagan king in Babylon: the fiery furnace in Daniel 3, and the lion's den in Daniel 6. The pagan kings refer to these deliverances as 'signs and wonders' in Daniel 4:2-3 and Daniel 6:27.

What about the New Testament?

On the day of Pentecost, Peter's sermon to the crowd quotes from Joel 2. He adapts the Old Testament text a little to read:

> ... I will show *wonders* in the heavens above and *signs* on the earth beneath ... (Acts 2:19).

He then goes on to speak of

> ... Jesus of Nazareth, a man attested to you by God with mighty works and *wonders and signs* which God did through him in your midst ... (Acts 2:22).

The Old Testament background suggests that this amounts to saying that the works of Jesus match in significance the events surrounding exodus from Egypt. The fourth Gospel refers most consistently to the 'signs' which Jesus did, the climactic one being, as in Peter's speech in Acts 2, his resurrection from the dead.

Signs and wonders and faith
Now if these are the signs and wonders which the Bible centrally proclaims, I want to ask what signs and wonders have to do with faith.

The first thing to notice is that in the Old Testament, faith involves *remembering the signs and wonders by which God redeemed his people.*

Moses tells the Israelites what they are to tell their children:

> You shall say to your son, 'We were Pharaoh's slaves in Egypt; and the Lord brought us out of Egypt with a mighty hand; and the Lord showed *signs and wonders*, great and grievous, against Egypt and against Pharaoh' (Deut 7:21-22).[20]

We hear the psalmists:

> I will call to mind the deeds of the Lord; yea I will remember thy *wonders* of old . . . Thou didst with thy arm redeem thy people (Ps 77:11, 15).[21]

In Old Testament times the signs and wonders that matter for faith in God are not contemporary miracles but the signs and wonders that accomplished the historical act of redemption.

Indeed unbelief is precisely a failure to remember those wonders:

> They forgot what he had done,
>   and the miracles he had shown them.
> In the sight of their fathers he wrought
>   marvels

> in the land of Egypt, in the fields of
> Zoan (Ps 78:11-12).[22]

In the New Testament the works of Jesus, supremely his resurrection, take the place of the exodus wonders. And *these* are the wonders that matter for New Testament faith. John wrote,

> Now Jesus did many other signs in
> the presence of the disciples, which
> are not written in this book; but *these
> are written that you may believe that
> Jesus is the Christ, the Son of God,*
> and that believing you may have life in
> his name (John 20:30-31).

In the Bible, therefore, the 'signs and wonders' that matter for true faith in God are those involved in God's historical acts of redemption.

A consequence of this is the fact that the desire for further signs and wonders is sinful and unbelieving:

> Some of the scribes and Pharisees said
> to him, 'Teacher we wish to see a sign
> from you'. But he answered them,
> 'An evil and adulterous generation
> seeks for a sign; but no sign shall be
> given to it except the sign of the
> prophet Jonah' (Matt 12:38-39).[23]

In John's Gospel this theme comes to a climax in the words addressed to Thomas, which come immediately before the words about the signs being *'written* that you may believe':

> Have you believed because you have seen me? Blessed are those who have not seen and yet believe (John 20:29).[24]

This is a very significant strand of New Testament teaching about signs and wonders. It is in each of the gospels several times. Sometimes it is the disciples, sometimes it is the Pharisees or the crowds who ask for a sign. Notice that they do not ask for a *wonder*, but a *sign*. There is no suggestion in the texts that they are interested in just seeing a miracle for its own sake. As they put it in John 6:30, their question is:

> Then what sign do you do, *that we may see, and believe you?*

We are bound to ask why the desire to see signs is so seriously repudiated by Jesus.

I think that the clearest answer is given by Jesus in the parable of the rich man and Lazarus (Luke 16:19-31). The rich man begged Abraham to send Lazarus back from the dead to warn his brothers of the reality of God's judgment.

> But Abraham said, 'They have Moses
> and the prophets; let them hear them'
> (Luke 16:29).

<u>That is, they have the word of God in the</u> Scriptures. <u>That is enough.</u>

> And he [the rich man] said, 'No,
> father Abraham; but if someone goes
> to them from the dead, they will
> repent ' (Luke 16:30).

That is, the Scriptures are not sufficient; they need a wonder to bring them to repentance.

> He [Abraham] said to him, 'If they do
> not hear Moses and the prophets,
> neither will they be convinced if one
> should rise from the dead'
> (Luke 16:31).

The purpose of the Bible's signs and wonders—*even the resurrection of Jesus*—is not to achieve what the word of God cannot achieve. Jesus says that what the word of God in the Scriptures does not achieve will *not* be achieved even by a resurrection.

The same point was made by the apostle Paul. The desire for further signs did not cease with the death and resurrection of Jesus. In 1 Corinthians we find that Paul defends the gospel, the proclaimed word of the cross, against the Jews who demand signs and the Greeks who seek wisdom. There he insists:

> I decided to know nothing among you
> except Jesus Christ and him crucified
> (1 Cor 2:2).

This, in contrast to the signs demanded by Jews and the philosophical wisdom sought by Greeks, he regarded as a 'demonstration of the Spirit and power' (1 Cor 1:22-23; 2:4). His purpose was

> ... that your faith might not rest in
> the wisdom of men but in the power
> of God (1 Cor 2:5).

Faith that rests in the power of God is created by God through the gospel which proclaims the death of Jesus Christ for our sins.[25]

The desire for *another* wonder to create faith, or strengthen faith, not only arises from sinful unbelief, but it would not lead to faith that rests on the power of God.

Why? Because the power of God which saves sinners is *not seen* in any contemporary miracle, no matter how marvelous, but only in the death of Christ on the cross. Any distraction from *that* display of God's power is just that—a distraction. Certainly (as we will see) Paul's ministry was, at times, accompanied by 'signs and wonders', but it is important to notice that precisely when his audience is attracted by these things he plays them down:

> Jews demand signs and Greeks seek wisdom, but we preach Christ crucified, a stumbling block to Jews, and folly to Gentiles, but to those who are called, both Jews and Greeks, Christ the power of God and the wisdom of God (1 Cor 1:22-24).

It may be argued from 2 Corinthians 12:12 that Paul did, after all, perform signs and wonders at Corinth. That may or may not be so (see endnote 28), but as with baptism (see 1 Cor 1:14-16), Paul indicates in 1 Corinthians 1 and 2 that it is neither here nor there. Evangelism as described in this context (with no mention of signs and wonders) is in no sense 'incomplete'. It is fully sufficient to lead to faith that rests in the power of God.

Signs and wonders and falsehood
What we have seen is that in the Bible the 'significant wonders'—the wonders that matter for faith—are the events surrounding the great redemptive acts of God. If these are not sufficiently wonderful for me, or if they are not sufficiently significant for me, then both Old and New Testaments judge me to be an unbeliever. Certainly John, as he wrote his Gospel, considered that his *record* of the signs that Jesus did would lead people to life-giving faith (John 20:30-31).

Are any other events in the Bible described as 'signs and wonders'?

The Old Testament anticipates that there will be *rival* signs and wonders. There will be false prophets whose characteristic will be that they will not call the people back to the historic redemptive acts of God, but will provide alternative signs and wonders.

> If a prophet arises among you, or a dreamer of dreams, and gives you *a sign or a wonder,* and the sign or wonder which he tells you comes to pass, and if he says, 'Let us go after other gods,' which you have not known, 'and let us serve them,' you shall not listen to the words of that prophet or to that dreamer of dreams; for the Lord your God is testing you, to know whether you love the Lord your God with all your heart and with all your soul (Deut 13:1-3).

Notice that these are not bogus signs and wonders. They are not fraudulent. Neither are they said to be satanic or demonic. The issue is not the character or the source of these wonders. Indeed in this case the text identifies God as the source ('the Lord your God is testing you')! The issue is that the prophet who performs them may lead you to a god you have not known, a god other than the God you know as 'the Lord your God who brought you out of the land of Egypt and redeemed you out of the house of bondage' (Deut 13:5). <u>Of course the false god will be called 'Yahweh'. He will be spoken of in terms that will make him sound like the Lord your God.</u> That is the danger of the false prophet.[26] But this false god is one who is known other than in the historical acts of redemption.

The New Testament speaks with even greater clarity and seriousness about rival signs and wonders that can lead astray. Jesus said,

> False Christs and false prophets will arise and show great *signs and wonders*, so as to lead astray, if possible, even the elect (Matt 24:24; Mark 13:22).

Notice again that <u>whoever these false prophets are, they must be very like the real thing if they come near to deceiving the elect.</u>

The sombre words of Paul strike the same note:

> The coming of the lawless one by the activity of Satan will be with all power and with pretended [or lying] *signs and wonders*, and with all wicked deception for those who are to perish, because they refused to love the truth and so be saved (2 Thess 2:9-10).

This is a theme which comes to its climactic expression with the second beast of Revelation 13:

> It works great *signs*, even making fire come down from heaven to earth in the sight of men; and by the *signs* which it is allowed to work in the presence of the [first] beast, it deceives those who dwell on the earth . . . (Rev 13:13-14).

To summarise so far: In the Bible there are broadly two kinds of events called 'signs and wonders'. On the one hand, there are the redemptive acts of God proclaimed by the Old and New Testaments. On the other hand, both Testaments warn forcefully that there will be rival and deceiving signs and wonders almost capable of deceiving even the elect, certainly capable of deceiving those who do not love the truth. The latter will look very like true prophecy or genuine Christianity. But most of its deceptive power will come from its impressive 'signs and wonders'.

Signs and wonders and the apostles and prophets

There are two other groups of events referred to in the Bible as 'signs and wonders'.

Firstly, in the Old Testament true prophecy is frequently accompanied by 'signs', and occasionally by 'signs and wonders'. Only twice is the latter expression used in association with true prophecy, and the striking thing is that the phenomena so described are not what we would call miracles. Isaiah describes himself and his children

Evangelical Ministry

as 'signs and wonders in Israel from the Lord of hosts' (Isa 8:18). The same prophet is said to have walked naked and barefoot for three years 'as a sign and a wonder' (Isa 20:3).[27] What made these phenomena 'wonders', it would seem, was the message signified by them.

There is one other group of events described by the Bible as 'signs and wonders'. These are the ones which receive most attention from John Wimber, but it seems crucial to me that the broader biblical background be kept in mind.

After the day of Pentecost, when Peter announced that God had once again done signs and wonders in the person and work of Jesus (Acts 2:19 and 22), Luke records that,

> fear came upon every soul; and many wonders and signs were done *through the apostles* (Acts 2:43).

Later he records,

> Now many signs and wonders were done among the people *by the hands of the apostles* (Acts 5:12).

At Iconium, Paul and Barnabas

> . . . remained for a long time, speaking boldly for the Lord, who bore witness to the word of his grace,

> granting signs and wonders to be done *by their hands* (Acts 14:3).

Such events were reported to the Jerusalem council:

> All the assembly kept silent, and they listened to Barnabas and Paul as they related what signs and wonders God had done *through them* among the Gentiles (Acts 15:12).

When Paul wrote to the Roman Christians he made reference to the same thing:

> I will not venture to speak of anything except what Christ has wrought *through me* to win obedience from the Gentiles, by word and deed, by the power of signs and wonders, by the power of the Holy Spirit, so that from Jerusalem and as far round as Illyricum I have fully preached the gospel of Christ . . . (Rom 15:19).

In 2 Corinthians 12 Paul makes a similar reference, although the irony of his argument in this context suggests that he might mean something rather different here:

> I have been a fool! You forced me to it, for I ought to have been

> commended by you. For I am not at all inferior to these superlative apostles, even though I am nothing. The *signs of an apostle* were performed among you in all patience, with signs and wonders and mighty works (2 Cor 12:11-12).[28]

Finally, these signs and wonders done by the hands of the apostles are referred to in Hebrews:

> It [the great salvation] was declared at first by the Lord, and it was attested to us *by those who heard him,* while God also bore witness by signs and wonders and various miracles and by gifts of the Holy Spirit distributed according to his own will (Heb 2:3-4).

Notice how consistently it is emphasised that these are *apostolic* phenomena. In Acts 4:29-30, therefore, it seems clear that those praying expect that God will continue to perform signs and wonders *by the hands of the apostles.*[29] The only other persons who are said to do signs and wonders in Acts are Stephen and Philip (Acts 6:8, 8:13).

Let us summarise. 'Signs and wonders' do not stop in the New Testament with the ascension of Jesus. The ministry of the apostles, and some closely associated with them, is also marked by 'signs and wonders'.

The question then is whether the signs and wonders associated with the apostles in the New Testament represent the norm for the age in which we live, between the first and second comings of Christ, or whether they are somehow part and parcel of the redemptive event itself.

The answer to this question depends on the role of the New Testament apostles, for the function of these signs and wonders in the New Testament does not seem to be to authenticate the *message* but the *messengers*. Their emphatic association with the *apostles* suggests this, as well as the reference to 'the signs *of an apostle*' (2 Cor 12:12). If these signs and wonders authenticated *the apostles*, and the apostles play a unique foundational role in God's purposes (Eph 2:20), it is a mistake to expect these signs and wonders today. And it is a mistake to understand contemporary phenomena as 'signs and wonders'.

John Wimber has come to the opposite conclusion. Indeed, that was not so much his conclusion as his starting point. Believing that the apostolic period was the norm for Christian experience, especially in terms of the signs and wonders, Wimber set out to find how such experiences could become part of his life and ministry.

I believe that the result has been a more serious aberration from New Testament Christianity than he started with. It is a version of Christianity in which the gospel is not sufficiently powerful to produce mature Christian faith, the Scriptures are not sufficiently revealing for the life of faithful obedience to God, the finished work of Christ is not sufficiently relevant for effective evangelism, and the hope of Christ's coming is not sufficiently comforting for those who are suffering. These are harsh words which I would prefer not to write. But I cannot see that the conclusion can be avoided. I will briefly enlarge on each of these points in the next chapter.

Chapter Four

SIGNS AND WONDERS AND EVANGELICAL MINISTRY

Is the gospel sufficiently powerful?

In John Wimber's theology, signs are understood to have a power which surpasses the power of the gospel. This is evident in the very term *power evangelism*, where the power is not that of the gospel: Evangelism which has the gospel, but not signs and wonders is *not* 'power evangelism'. True, Wimber admits that he 'would not deny' that the gospel has intrinsic power.[30] And no doubt, if asked, he would affirm it, but it does not have a central place in his theology. The keys given to the church are 'spiritual insights and authority',[31] not the gospel. 'In order to enter the warfare, we must correctly understand power and authority in the kingdom',[32] which is something other than the gospel. What people need is something over and above the gospel.[33] In evangelistic methods without signs and wonders (what Paul calls 'deciding to know nothing among you except Jesus Christ and him crucified'), Wimber says many people who make decisions for Christ 'do not encounter God's power, and thus frequently do not move on to a mature faith . . . there is something inadequate about their conversion experience . . .'[34]

This is not evangelical Christianity. John Wimber's theology frequently fails to see the power of God in the gospel. Indeed he describes the gospel rationally explained as 'natural', while the 'power encounter' is 'supernatural'! The gospel is

> ... a rational explanation [that] must be added to a transrational experience, the natural to the supernatural, for the most forceful advance of the kingdom of God.[35]

He quotes C Peter Wagner:

> When the gospel first penetrates a region, if we don't go in with an understanding of and use of the supernatural power of the Holy Spirit, we just don't make much headway .. .[36]

It is quite clear that for Wimber the gospel is less than 'the supernatural power of the Holy Spirit'.

Any theology that often seems to forget that the gospel is the power of God cannot be described as evangelical.

It may be objected that signs and wonders for Wimber are no more an addition to the gospel than are the rational arguments often advanced by Evangelicals to support the truth of the gospel, or the godly life of Christians which enhances the credibility of the gospel.

The difference is that rational arguments, or Christian conduct, are not (or should not be) presented as 'the power of the Holy Spirit'. These things clear away barriers to hearing the gospel, but in no way make conversion more complete. If a person becomes a Christian without hearing rational arguments, or without seeing godly Christians, we do not think that 'there is something inadequate about their conversion experience'.

In many ways the wonders seem to have displaced the gospel. And so we find that a whole book is written on evangelism, with detailed attention to signs and wonders, but no discussion of the content or the power of the gospel. Evangelism and conversion to Christ can apparently take place without the gospel at all. At least the gospel is not at the heart of what Wimber thinks of when he speaks of evangelism. Here is one account:

> One day a group of our young people approached a stranger in a parking lot. Soon they were praying over him, and he fell to the ground. By the time he got up, the stranger was converted. He is now a member of our church.[37]

Whereas evangelicals have been motivated by the centrality of the gospel to train Christians in helpful techniques for communicating the gospel, Wimber provides training in techniques for praying for healing. He teaches Christians how to offer an apologetic for healing.[38] He sends out teams on door-to-door praying for healing.[39]

As I said at the beginning, prayer for the sick is right and important, but it must not be given a significance that displaces the gospel.

Are the Scriptures sufficiently revealing?

One of the keys to the renewal of powerful Christianity which Wimber teaches is obedience to God. The difficulty is that he hardly ever means by that obedience to the word of God in Scripture. The Scriptures are not sufficiently revealing for the obedience of which Wimber is speaking. Of course he believes in the *authority* of Scripture. The issue here is not the authority, but the *sufficiency* of Scripture.

He explains how he 'hears' God like this:

> For the reader who has never had a vision or supernaturally 'heard' God in this fashion, I did not *physically* hear God speak. I experienced more of an impression, a spiritual sense of God speaking to me.[40]

Nowhere in the New Testament are Christians taught to expect or seek messages from God in that fashion.

But for John Wimber, hearing God through hunches (which, as he admits, often turn out to be wrong) is essential. The stories John Wimber tells nearly always involve, as an essential feature, his 'hearing' a message from God. Without such messages there would be no stories to tell.

This is perhaps the most essential element in John Wimber's distinctive teaching, but it has no basis in the New Testament's teaching about the Christian life. We know of no one in the New Testament who got messages from God through hunches (Wimber's term), let alone hunches that were often wrong. Certainly nowhere are Christians taught to look for such hunches.

It is my distinct impression that *these* hunches 'from God' to a large extent displace the Scriptures as the means of hearing God's word.

This is therefore a version of the Christian life in which the Scriptures are not sufficiently revealing for the most obedient Christian life. *Sola scriptura* (Bible alone) is not one of its mottos. If I believe (as I do) that the Bible is the fully sufficient Word of God for faithful Christian living, then I cannot accept the teaching of John Wimber. He is asking us to expect, or be 'open' to God doing what God has not promised to do. This is an 'openness' to which the Bible does not call us. It must therefore be recognised as a departure from evangelical Christianity.

Is the work of Christ sufficiently relevant?

In 'power evangelism' the fundamental 'givenness' of the gospel as a proclamation of what God *has done* in Christ is undervalued:

> In programmatic evangelism, Christians might be fearful as they speak, but they are not unsure about *what* they are going to say before opening their mouths. In power evangelism, Christians are consciously under God's commission and control . . . they cannot depend on a prepackaged message . . . In power evangelism, God speaks and then we act.[41]

Contrast that with the apostle:

> Now brothers, I want to remind you of the gospel I preached to you, which you received and on which you have taken your stand. By this gospel you are saved, if you hold firmly to the word I preached to you. Otherwise you have believed in vain. For what I received I passed on to you as of first importance: that Christ died for our sins . . . (1 Cor 15:1-3).

Evangelical Christianity has always taken its stand on the received gospel of the New Testament Scriptures, and proclaimed that 'prepackaged' message. John Wimber's point is that such evangelism is often *incomplete* because it lacks demonstration of the kingdom of God in signs and wonders. In other words, *the finished work of*

Evangelical Ministry

Christ proclaimed in the gospel message is not sufficient for the best evangelism.

The power of evangelical ministry is that God has revealed in the Bible *what* he purposes to do, and *how* he purposes to do it. And God keeps his promises! Evangelical ministry is shaped by this reality, not by an expectation that God will do things he has not promised to do.

It is important to understand why signs are necessary in Wimber's view. They provide a solid ground for assurance. 'Power encounters authenticate conversion experiences in a way that mere intellectual assent does not. This gives new Christians confidence about their conversion, a solid foundation for the rest of their lives'.[42] In other words, *the finished work of Christ proclaimed in the gospel message is not sufficient for fully confident Christian faith*.

The New Testament and church history should teach us that such additions to the finished work of Christ are really subtractions from it, for they deny its sufficiency.

Wimber's theology seems perilously close to proclaiming another gospel, from another source.

Is the hope of Christ's coming sufficiently comforting?

Although Wimber believes in and speaks of Christ's return, it seems to me that this hope is displaced in his teaching by hope for healing here and now. He quotes Hebrews 11:1,

> Now faith is the assurance of things hoped for and the conviction of things not seen . . .

and understands the 'things hoped for' as healing! His question is, 'Do you believe that Jesus will do it now?'[43] When people are not healed in answer to prayer he comforts them with 'maybe you will be healed when prayed for next time'. And if they are not, he tells them that 'that is sometimes the way the Lord works before he heals'.[44] Compare the New Testament comfort:

> I consider that the sufferings of this present time are not worth comparing with the glory that is to be revealed to us (Rom 8:18).

Again:

> We rejoice in our hope of sharing the glory of God. More than that, we rejoice in our sufferings, knowing that suffering produces endurance, and endurance produces character, and character produces hope, and hope does not disappoint us, because God's love has been poured into our hearts through the Holy Spirit which has been given to us. For while we were yet helpless, at the right time Christ died for the ungodly (Rom 5:2-6).

Chapter Five

THE MIRACULOUS AND THE CHRISTIAN LIFE

The main point that I have attempted to make so far is that the significance given by John Wimber to various occurrences by calling them 'signs and wonders' is mistaken, and has led him away from evangelical Christianity.

Some questions, however, remain. What *are* the phenomena which Wimber describes as 'signs and wonders'? What place should they have in our Christian lives, or in our evangelism? How should we respond when confronted with these events, or accounts of them?

To reflect on these questions I will turn attention to four New Testament passages that are frequently referred to by John Wimber.

Matthew 28:18-20

> And Jesus came and said to them, 'All authority in heaven and on earth has been given to me. Go therefore and make disciples of all nations, baptising them in the name of the Father and of the Son and of the Holy Spirit, teaching them to observe all that I have commanded you; and lo, I am with you always, to the close of the age'.

If, as I have argued, the phenomena associated with John Wimber's ministry should not be called 'signs and wonders', he would still argue that they are *a necessary part of Christian discipleship*. The argument is based on these concluding words of Matthew's Gospel, often called the Great Commission.

Wimber's interpretation of the Great Commission goes like this. Jesus' last command, which has validity 'to the close of the age', was to make *disciples*. How do you make disciples? By baptising them, and by teaching them to observe *all that Jesus commanded his first disciples*. What did Jesus command his first disciples? Wimber finds the answer in Matthew 10. There Jesus commanded his disciples to preach the gospel, to heal the sick, raise the dead, cleanse lepers and to cast out demons (vv. 7-8).

The problem, overlooked by Wimber, is that in verses 5 and 6 of Matthew 10 Jesus also commanded his disciples:

> Go *nowhere among the Gentiles,* and
> enter no town of the Samaritans, but
> go rather to the lost sheep of the house
> of Israel.

It is quite clear from the rest of the New Testament that 'all that I have commanded you' in Matthew 28:20 does not include the commands of Matthew 10:5-6! But Wimber wants to insist that it includes the commands of Matthew 10:7-8. Is he right?

One way of answering the question is to read the rest of the New Testament. *Do we find the apostles teaching people to heal the sick, raise the dead, cleanse lepers, and cast out demons?* Neither in the book of Acts nor in the Epistles do we find any such teaching. The closest approach to such teaching is James 5:13-18, where those who are suffering are encouraged to pray, and those who are sick are encouraged to call the elders of the church to pray over them. This is important, but it seems that either the Great Commission was not obeyed in New Testament times, or Jesus did not mean what John Wimber understands him to mean.

What, then, did Jesus mean by 'all that I have commanded you'?

The words are reminiscent of certain Old Testament expressions which refer to the totality of God's revelation of his requirements to the people of Israel at Mount Sinai.[45] Jesus' commands to those who follow him are the fulfillment of the demands of the Old Testament (see Matt 5:17). 'All that I have commanded you' refers to the totality of Jesus' teaching.

What about Matthew 10?

God commanded Moses to do many specific things that had to do with the particular occasion, but these were not timeless commands for all Israelites at all times.[46] Likewise, the mission of the disciples in Matthew 10 had the limited objective of preparing the way for Jesus coming to those specific parts of the country. Many features had to do with that specific purpose (see vv. 9-15).

It is clear from the rest of the New Testament and from the immediate context that verses 7 and 8 of Matthew 10 are no more essential aspects of discipleship today than verses 5 and 6, or verses 9 to 15.

It is interesting to notice that there is a striking difference between Jesus' commissionings of his disciples for missions before his resurrection (Matt 10; Mark 6; Luke 9, 10) and after:

> After his resurrection, Jesus—according to the most ancient Greek texts—gives no mandate to undertake a healing ministry. He does tell his disciples to teach all nations and to baptise in his name (Matt 28:19, 20). He does speak of repentance and forgiveness being preached to all nations (Luke 24:47). He does promise the authority of the Spirit to forgive and retain sins (John 20:22, 23). But he does not re-invest his disciples with a commission to do miraculous healing and resuscitation.[47]

The Great Commission, therefore, does not give us the terms in which to understand the phenomena associated with John Wimber.

Mark 16:15-18

> And he [Jesus] said to them, 'Go into all the world and preach the gospel to the whole creation. He who believes and is baptised will be saved; but he who does not believe will be condemned. And these signs will accompany those who believe: in my name they will cast out demons; they will speak in new tongues; they will pick up serpents, and if they drink any deadly thing, it will not hurt them; they will lay their hands on the sick, and they will recover.

This passage is remarkable. It provides the strongest support for John Wimber's interpretation of discipleship. It is the one passage which insists that these phenomena *will* be part of the normal Christian life, and cannot be limited to the apostles. It is also the most striking passage in the list of miracles it predicts.

Two points need to be made.

Firstly, these verses are almost certainly not part of the original Gospel of Mark. They are not present in the most ancient Greek texts. Translations usually make this clear. They were probably composed some time in the second century AD to round off the apparently abrupt ending of the Gospel at verse 8 of chapter 16. Another shorter attempt to 'complete' the Gospel is also known, and is indicated in most translations. So much uncertainty surrounds the verses quoted that it would be wrong to base any doctrine or practice upon them.

Secondly, you cannot have your cake and eat it too. If Mark 16:15-18 is accepted as Scripture, it must be taken seriously in *all* that it says. If believers 'drink any deadly thing, it *will not hurt them*'. When they lay hands on the sick, 'they *will recover*'. The promises are so out of character with the rest of the New Testament, and so inconsistent with experience (even John Wimber's experience, I think) that we are not surprised to find that they are of dubious authenticity.

This passage, therefore, does not help us at all to understand the 'signs and wonders' of John Wimber, and should not be used by him to support his case.

John 14:12

> Truly, truly I say to you, he who
> believes in me will also do the works
> that I do; and greater things than these
> will he do, because I go to the Father.

Are John Wimber's 'signs and wonders' the 'greater works' here promised by Jesus, or perhaps 'the works that I do' which believers in Jesus will also do?

Evangelical Ministry

It is important to notice what Jesus did *not* say. He did not say 'He who believes in me will also do the *signs* that I do', but 'He who believes in me will also do the *works* that I do'. In John's Gospel the word 'sign' always refers to miracles. 'Works' is a more general word which includes all of Jesus' activity, including his words (see John 14:10).

> It includes what we would call the 'natural' activities of Jesus as well as the 'supernatural'. It reminds us that these are all of a piece, that Jesus' whole life was consistently spent in doing the will of God and in accomplishing his purpose. Not only in the miracles, but in all his life he was showing forth God's glory.[48]

For example in John 6:28 the people ask Jesus, 'What must we do to be doing the works of God?' He replied, 'This is the work of God, that you believe in him whom he has sent' (John 6:29).

Jesus' words, therefore, do not mean that believers will do the same *miracles* as Jesus, and greater ones, but that the *works* of Jesus, which are the works of God, will be carried on through believers—and in an even greater way. The reason that believers will do 'greater things' is given: 'because I go to the Father'. That is to say, what God will do through believers after Jesus has completed his work on earth, climaxing of course in his death, will be greater than the works of Jesus before his death, resurrection and ascension.

There is an indication of what is meant by this in some very similar words spoken by Jesus earlier in this Gospel:

> The Father loves the Son, and shows him all that he himself is doing; and *greater works than these* will he show him, that you may marvel. For as the Father raises the dead and gives them life, so also *the Son gives life* to whom he will. The Father judges no one, but has given all judgment to the Son, that all may honour the Son, even as they honour the Father. He who does not honour the Son does not honour the Father who sent him. Truly, truly, I say to you, *he who hears my word and believes him who sent me, has eternal life;* he does not come into judgment, but has passed from death to life (John 5:20-24).

What are the greater works (v. 20)? People passing from death to life (vv. 21 and 24)! How does that happen? By hearing the word of Jesus, and believing the one who sent him (v. 24).

The promise of John 14:12, therefore, has little to do with miracles. John Wimber's 'signs and wonders' are not the 'greater things' promised here.

Evangelical Ministry

They are better explained in terms of our next passage.

1 Corinthians 12-14

From the evidence available in chapters 12 to 14 of 1 Corinthians, phenomena comparable to those encouraged by John Wimber seem to have been present in the church at Corinth. In my opinion, it is these chapters of the New Testament that most clearly point to a proper assessment and response to these things.

Notice first that <u>when Paul refers to the apparently miraculous phenomena in the Corinthian church (1 Cor 12:8-10) he does *not* call them 'signs and wonders'</u>. He seems to limit that expression to occurrences which authenticate an apostle (or purport to authenticate the antichrist).

Secondly, notice that these things (and, frankly, we have little idea what some of them were) are discussed by Paul because they were *already* part of Corinthian church life, and he writes to instruct them about their proper use. Historical research suggests that at least many, perhaps all, of the phenomena under discussion were practised widely in first century non-Christian religions. There is no evidence that where such phenomena were not part of church life Paul would encourage their introduction. Look, for example at the list of 'gifts' in Romans 12:6-8.

The list in 1 Corinthians 12:8-10, therefore, is not in any sense a definitive list of 'gifts of the Spirit'. It is a list of phenomena already occurring in the Corinthian church, which they are to understand and use in a particular way.

Thirdly, the basic thrust of Paul's teaching to the Corinthians is that these things must be thought of by them as *gifts given for the common good* (1 Cor 12:4 and 7). The Corinthians had a tendency to forget that whatever they had was God's *gift* to them. Earlier in the letter Paul wrote:

> What have you that you did not receive? If then you received it, why do you boast as if it were not a gift (1 Cor 4:7).

In other words, in 1 Corinthians 12 Paul is not teaching about the kind of things the Spirit *characteristically* gives, but about how the Corinthians must understand the things they *have*.

Finally, chapter 14 makes clear the 'common good' which is to control the use of these things. It is 'upbuilding and encouragement and consolation . . . building up the church . . . that all may learn and all may be encouraged' (1 Cor 14:3, 5, 12, 31), which is achieved by intelligible speech (see especially vv. 6-12).

This is entirely consistent with what we saw in 1 Corinthians 1 and 2, where the power that matters in evangelism was located in the *word* of the gospel. So it is that the power which builds up faith in God is located, according to 1 Corinthians 14, in intelligible *words*.

Evangelical Ministry

How should we understand and respond to the phenomena associated with John Wimber's ministry? My opinion is that we should follow Paul's lead in responding to the Corinthians:

1. Don't call them 'signs and wonders'. That is to give them a wrong significance. In particular, healing in answer to prayer should not be exalted above other answers to prayer, such as patience in suffering.
2. Don't be concerned about not being like the Corinthians. There is nothing normative about what went on in the Corinthian church! The Bible does *not* teach that the phenomena at Corinth are important or even desirable.
3. If you find yourself among Christians who practise the kind of things mentioned in 1 Corinthians 12 to 14, try to encourage the upbuilding of Christian faith through the word of God intelligibly spoken.
4. If you are a Christian who practises these things, carefully study Paul's teaching, and keep your priorities right. Do not forget that the sword of the Spirit is the *word* of God.

Chapter Six

CONCLUSION: TWO WAYS TO LEAVE

Since God has made himself and his ways with us known in the Bible, there are two errors which must be avoided.

The first is *not believing that God will do what he has promised.* We are often good at knowing what God has revealed about his purposes and his ways in the Bible. But it is our actions which demonstrate whether we *believe* it. I know that the Bible says the gospel is God's power to save people (Rom 1:16). Whether I believe that or not will be shown by my actions. I know that the Bible teaches the sufferings of this present time are not worth comparing to the glory that is to be revealed to us (Rom 8:18). Whether I believe it or not will be shown by my responses to my suffering today.

The second error is *believing that God will do what he has not promised.* This is sometimes described as 'being open to God doing unusual things', which gives it the appearance of being great faith in God. But it is not the faith to which the Bible calls us. Nowhere does the Bible call us to be 'open' to what God has not promised.

John Wimber perceives the first error in much modern Christianity. I suspect that he is right. But it will not do to correct the first error by making the second error.

Nor will it do to perceive the second error in John Wimber's teaching, and be content to remain with the first error!

I hope that John Wimber's visit to Australia will cause us to radically review our Christian lives and ministries in the light of the Bible, to be renewed in our confidence that the weak and foolish word of the cross is the very power and wisdom of God (it is a *supernatural* word), to be moved more to the 'supernatural' activity of letting our requests be made known to our heavenly Father, to see more clearly the love of God demonstrated to us 'supernaturally' in the death of his Son. If these are the indirect consequences of the controversy that will result from John Wimber's time here, then for that we can thank God.

Addendum

METHODS OF ARGUMENT

It is important to see the kinds of argument that John Wimber advances. Many of them are invalid, although they have some rhetorical and emotional force.

Argument from results
Much of Wimber's case is built on argument from results. He notes, for example, that 'an estimated 70 percent of all church growth is among Pentecostal and charismatic groups'.[49] Quoting C Peter Wagner:

> I began discovering that the churches that were far outgrowing all the others were the Pentecostal churches . . . What I am seeing is that worldwide there is a remarkably close relationship between growth of the churches today and the healing ministry . . .[50]

Wimber's observation of the American scene is that 'most American churches lacked both power encounters and dramatic growth so common in other parts of the world'.[51]

The problem with this kind of argument is twofold:

1. It makes church growth the measure of truth. That cannot be correct. Apart from the fact that there is no biblical basis for it, there is no sense to it. I might as well argue from the remarkable growth of the Mormon church for the validity of the Book of Mormon, or from the success of the Jehovah's Witnesses in Sydney against the deity of Christ.
2. It assumes that two facts (church growth and 'power encounters') are linked as cause and effect. This does not follow, as a moment's reflection on the two examples just given will show. Is it non-belief in the deity of Christ that accounts for the growth of the Jehovah's Witnesses? I suspect that there are several factors that account for the striking growth of charismatic churches in many places, *one* of which *may be* the emphasis on 'signs'.

If Wimber's theology of signs and wonders is true, the results in terms of growing churches are not evidence of that. Our longing to see people converted to Christ and churches grow is right and good, and accounts for much of the appeal of Wimber's message. It promises what we rightly long for. But is the message *true* according to the Bible?

Non-biblical categories

A method of argument that pervades John Wimber's teaching, with serious consequences, is along the following lines.

From his observations and experience Wimber develops a category of experience for which he invents (or takes up from someone else) a term. Important examples are 'power evangelism', 'power encounter' and 'divine appointment'. These terms are not biblical, which is not itself a problem. The problem is that the *categories* are not biblical. However, Wimber proceeds to put biblical (and other historical) events into these categories.[52] This seems to validate the categories, but in fact it distorts the Bible (and perhaps other history).

For example, by categorising some New Testament evangelism as 'power evangelism', this is distinguishing it from other evangelism in the New Testament that does not fit the invented category. So Wimber supposes that Paul's evangelism at Corinth was 'power evangelism', but not so at Athens.[53] The New Testament itself, however, does not draw this distinction. There are not, in the New Testament, two *kinds* of evangelism. Indeed in at least one place (1 Cor 2:1-5) Paul describes his evangelism *apart from signs and wonders* (see 1 Cor 2:2-3, and 1:22-24) as a 'demonstration of the Spirit and power' (1 Cor 2:4). Wimber, in this way, has imposed categories on the New Testament which are foreign to New Testament thought, and distort it.

False generalisations about the New Testament

By a selective reading of the New Testament, and reading back of these invented categories, Wimber comes up with false generalisations about New Testament Christianity. Take this statement, for example:

> Clearly the early Christians had an openness to the power of the Spirit, which resulted in signs and wonders and church growth. If we want to be like the early church, we too need to open to the Holy Spirit's power.[54]

The New Testament nowhere makes such a statement about the early Christians. To judge from some of the rebukes in the Epistles, many of them were open to things other than the Holy Spirit! They were not, in other words, so unlike us. Certainly nowhere does the New Testament relate signs and wonders or church growth to their 'openness'. Such an imaginative view of New Testament Christians can come only from a very selective reading and the imposition of ideas.

Likewise we find the following statement, based on 1 Corinthians 14:23-25:[55]

> In the New Testament, outsiders were afraid because they did not

> know what would happen to them if they moved in among Christians. They could be consumed by God's power; their secret sins could be revealed; healing could come on them; demons could be expulsed.[56]

How has Wimber concluded that that is how it was in New Testament times? Nowhere does the New Testament tell us so. The view has been imposed on his reading of the New Testament, probably by generalising imaginatively from statements like Acts 5:13.

These are not isolated examples, but typical. What Wimber sets out to demonstrate is that his theology of signs and wonders is biblical and normative. <u>It is clear, however, that he has *assumed* that his experiences, and his interpretations of them, correspond to the New Testament. The New Testament texts are understood in the light of that assumption.</u>

Blind spot in reading the New Testament

Because Wimber has imposed this understanding drawn from his interpreted experience on the New Testament, he appears to have a serious blind spot. The New Testament has much to say about the dangers of signs and wonders—and their dispensability (see chapter 3 above). This teaching is overlooked by Wimber.

On page 60 of *Power Evangelism*, for example, he treats Paul's evangelistic methods at Corinth. In

Athens, according to Wimber's reading of Acts 17, Paul had used eloquent argument, 'with the results that "a *few* men became followers of Paul and believed"'.⁵⁷ These 'meagre results' speak against Paul's preaching at Athens being used as a model of evangelism, says Wimber. At Paul's next stop, Corinth, we are told by Wimber that *many* people in this city believed. Consistent with his argument from results, he seeks an explanation of this in terms of Paul's evangelistic methods. The answer is found in 1 Corinthians 2:4, where Paul refers to his evangelistic work at Corinth as a demonstration of the Spirit's power. So at Athens it was 'programmatic evangelism', but in Corinth it was 'power evangelism'!

Wimber's reading of 1 Corinthians 2:1-5 actually inverts the meaning of the text. Paul has already made the point that he does *not* use 'power evangelism' (to use Wimber's term in Wimber's sense):

> Jews demand signs and Greeks seek wisdom, *but* we preach Christ crucified, a stumbling block to Jews and folly to Gentiles, but to those who are called, both Jews and Greeks, Christ the power of God and the wisdom of God (1 Cor 1:22-24).

For Paul the power of God *is* the word of the cross (1 Cor 1:18; cf. Rom 1:16). His point is that *what appears weak to the Jews and foolish to the*

Evangelical Ministry

Greeks, that is the gospel message, is itself the power of God. He makes the point as forcefully as possible in 1 Corinthians 2:1-5, by asserting that in his evangelism he 'decided to know *nothing* among you except Jesus Christ and him crucified'. *That* was a demonstration of the Spirit and power. And he eschews other ways of demonstrating power, precisely in order that 'your faith might rest . . . in the power of God'. Wimber has *reversed* Paul's meaning.

This is not a matter of pedantic exegetical precision. What the apostle Paul refused to say, Wimber insists on saying. This reflects a different understanding of the gospel and of evangelism from that of the New Testament.

Wimber's treatment of John's Gospel shows the same blind spot. He refers to Jesus challenging Philip to believe in him on the basis of his miracles (John 14:10-11),[58] but misses the important strand of John's Gospel which highlights the value of faith *without* sight. See especially the words that were addressed to Thomas in John 20:29: 'Blessed are those who have *not* seen and yet have believed'.

Again these are not isolated examples, but indications of a writer more dominated by his interpretation of his own experience than by the Bible. It appears that the Bible has been subordinated to his interpreted experience.

Misinterpretations because of the invented categories

Because the categories which Wimber has set up are not themselves biblical categories of thought, and because they are imposed on his reading of the Bible, he falls into many other gross misinterpretations.

'All Christians are commanded to seek the Holy Spirit (see Eph 5:18) regardless of how that experience is labelled'.[59] But the New Testament nowhere commands anyone to *seek* the Holy Spirit.[60] The command of Ephesians 5:18 is 'be filled with (or fulfilled in) the Spirit'. This refers to a state of life in which the believer is told to live. Wimber's interest in experiences which can be obtained by 'seeking' them leads him to see the 'command to seek' where it is not present. We are told that 'John the Baptist, Jesus, and Peter all taught that we should seek to be overwhelmed by the Spirit'.[61] What they actually taught was a *promise*, the condition of which was not *seeking* (see Luke 3:16; Acts 1:5 and 2:38 respectively). If there is a condition, it is repentance (Acts 2:38). Furthermore, Wimber refers this 'experience' of the Holy Spirit narrowly to 'gifts and power'. That is simply because his own experience is again shaping his understanding. No careful reading of the New Testament could yield such a narrow view of the Christian's experience of the Holy Spirit.

One other striking example of Wimber's imposition of foreign categories on the New Testament is found on page 55 of *Power*

Evangelical Ministry 67

Evangelism. Here he refers to D Martyn Lloyd-Jones' observation that in the book of Acts 'in every instance where we are told either that the Spirit came upon these men or that they were filled with the Spirit, you will find that it was in order to bear a witness and a testimony' (to Jesus). The obvious conclusion is that these experiences of the Holy Spirit were linked to the proclamation of the gospel. Wimber's conclusion (implied) is that signs and wonders are all but essential for evangelism. He reaches this by imposing the view that being filled with the Spirit must be linked to performing signs and wonders. This is not a New Testament view. Instead of seeing, as did Lloyd-Jones, the link made in Acts (Spirit and evangelism), he imposes another (Spirit, signs and wonders, evangelism). But that is not what the text of Scripture says or implies.

Exaggerated claims?
A third aspect of Wimber's method of argument that has considerable effect is the collection of remarkable stories that <u>illustrate (and presumably are intended to validate) his message</u>. The reader of Wimber's writings is not, of course, in a position to check the accuracy of his anecdotes. Neither is this necessarily important. One of the unfortunate effects of the charismatic movement has been the linking of bad theology to the 'miraculous', so that those who reject the theology have often felt, for example, that prayer and hope for healing is 'suspect'. Evangelical Christians should understand

the sovereignty of God in all things, and know that it is right to bring all our cares to him in prayer 'because he cares for you' (1 Peter 5:7). To reject Wimber's theology is not to say that all his anecdotes must be untrue.

However, it should be pointed out that there are indications that at least sometimes he is given to exaggeration. For example, describing the life of his church in California, he says, 'The blind see; the lame walk; the deaf hear. Cancer is disappearing'.[62] A few pages later he claims, with reference to John 14:12, that these are even greater miracles than Jesus did.

There are other claims that are probably exaggerations. The claim that invariably Christians for whom Wimber prays are 'filled with the Spirit',[63] in his sense of the term, is an obvious candidate.

Acts normative?

One important question that Bible readers need to ask when reading many parts of the Bible is: Are these events unique or normative? So, for example: Is Moses' experience at the burning bush a model for the believer's experience of God, or a demonstration of the unique place of Moses in the purposes of God? It is not difficult to demonstrate that in this case the rest of the Old Testament understands accounts like that in Exodus 3 in the latter sense. This is not 'dispensationalism', unless being open to the possibility of historical particularity is 'dispensationalism'.

The question when applied to the book of Acts marks one of the points of controversy raised again by Wimber. 'The gap between the early disciples' experience as they spread the gospel of the kingdom of God, and what my congregation experienced'[64] is a great problem for Wimber, mainly because he has *assumed* (he certainly has not argued the case) that Acts must be typical. So Acts 1:8 is about *everyone*.[65] You don't have to be a 'dispensationalist' to say that it is not *necessarily* so.

The problem is that Wimber's present experience is now *made* to accord with the book of Acts by imposing his interpretation of his experience on the book of Acts in the ways that we have seen. And if, as I believe, the wonders of Acts are far more impressive than anything happening today, this is no longer appreciated. The wonders recorded in the Bible are downgraded to match their supposed equivalents today.

Opponents not understood

A final problem to be mentioned here is that Wimber seems to take little account of opposing viewpoints. Those that he mentions are normally 'straw men'. Most frequently he cites opposing views second hand, from those who hold his own view.

Furthermore, notable authorities are cited to support this point or that, with no evident awareness that many of them would fundamentally disagree with Wimber's views.

Part Two

PAUL, THE MIRACULOUS AND MINISTRY

by

Paul Barnett

Chapter Seven

THE CHALLENGE TO PAUL'S MINISTRY

In this section I wish to measure two basic assertions made by John Wimber in his *Power Evangelism* against the teaching of Paul in his second letter to the Corinthians.

The first assertion is that the 'signs and wonders' evident in the New Testament continued into history and are readily available today in the work of evangelism. It is Mr Wimber's belief that since the kingdom of God inaugurated by Jesus was initially marked by 'signs and wonders', the ongoing proclamation of the kingdom should continue to be characterised by such phenomena. Christ's mission and ours is to attack the kingdom of Satan by proclamation of the gospel in the Holy Spirit's demonstration of 'signs and wonders' (see, in particular, chapter 1 and appendices A and B).

His second, and closely related, claim is that most evangelism in the western world is 'programmic', verbal in character and directed at the mind. This European-style evangelism is made ineffective by the secular and materialistic world-view dominant in the West. Evangelism in the third world, however, is said to be characterised by supernatural phenomena, by 'signs and wonders', by 'power'. The clear inference is that 'programmic', verbal evangelism is powerless and that those who exercise such ministries are powerless.

John Wimber's writings, itinerant lecturing and local church ministry are remarkably influential. His powerfully stated views, which claim the support of a number of influential Christian leaders, are shaking both the structure and the foundation of long-held evangelical beliefs. It would be unwise to dismiss lightly the doctrines taught by Mr Wimber.

I intend to examine these two interrelated assertions in light of Paul's second letter to the Corinthians. We will focus on five brief passages.

Paul and the superlative apostles

In about AD55 the church in Corinth was visited by a group of men who referred to themselves as 'apostles of Christ' and 'ministers of Christ' (11:13,23). They had come, in all probability, from Jerusalem on a judaising mission (11:22), to bring the Corinthian Christians under the Mosaic covenant. This is to be inferred from Paul's defence of the new covenant of Christ and the Spirit against the claims of the now superseded covenant of Moses (3:1-18). Paul's description of this group as 'ministers of righteousness' (11:15) implies that righteousness associated with law-keeping was fundamental to their mission. Paul's complaint that these persons have trespassed into his sphere of ministry is strongly suggestive of the Jerusalem Missionary Summit in AD47, when it was solemnly agreed that Paul's apostolate was to Gentiles and the apostolate of James, Cephas and John was to Jews (Gal 2:7-9). Thus, in breach of the Jerusalem Agreement, these judaising missionaries had invaded territory given to Paul.

What has this to do with John Wimber's ministry? The common element is *power*. Mr. Wimber is pointing to a ministry which, by its *power*-component, exceeds other merely verbal or 'programmic' ministries. The newly-arrived ministers in Corinth specifically compared their ministry with Paul's (10:12) and declared theirs to be superior to his (11:5; 12:11). The superiority claimed by them appears to be located in the manifestation by them of supernatural power, including 'signs and wonders'. Paul comments:

> I was not at all inferior to these superlative apostles (literally *hyper*-apostles) . . . The signs of a(n) . . . apostle were performed among you . . . signs, wonders and mighty works (12:12).

Paul's references to 'visions and revelations' (12:1) suggests, in the context of the letter, that the newcomers were also basing their claim to superiority over Paul on such things. His description of being 'caught up into the third heaven/paradise . . . in/out of the body' (12:2-3) indicates that claims, which sound so bizarre to us, were being made by these new ministers. During such extraterrestrial 'flights' were heard 'things which cannot be told, which man may not utter' (12:4). Paul's impersonal, distant and somewhat sarcastic manner of describing these phenomena indicates on the one hand that he made no ministry claims based on such experiences, whereas, on the other hand his opponents pointed specifically to these things to support and legitimate their claims.

His earlier comment, 'If we are beside ourselves, it is for God' (5:13), referring apparently to ecstatic speech and activities, is likewise a reference both to Paul's and his opponents' behaviour. Their 'ecstasy' presumably arose out of hearing 'unutterable' words when 'caught up into Paradise' (12:2-4) and was, in all probability, expressed in some form of strange speech. Their claim to legitimacy in ministry was based on such phenomena. Paul's ecstasy may have been the glossolalia to which he referred in his first letter (14:18-19). However, Paul refused to use this to legitimate his ministry.

It is clear, therefore, that Paul's opponents were pointing to signs, wonders, mighty powers and to certain mystical, paranormal activities to validate their ministries and, at the same time, to invalidate Paul's.

Clearly this has application to the teachings of John Wimber. There can be no doubt that for him true ministry is *power* evangelism, that is, proclamation demonstrated to be *powerful* by the manifestation of 'signs and wonders'. Evangelism which is not accompanied by such phenomena is therefore *powerless,* weak. This, as it happens, is

Paul, the Miraculous and Ministry

exactly what the newcomers said about Paul's ministry. His ministry was, they claimed, *insufficient* (2:16; 3:4-6); their's was powerfully triumphant (cf. 2:14). His ministry, verbal as it was (or 'programmatic' to use Mr Wimber's word) was worldly, weak and foolish (10:4,10; 11:7,16,21). Their ministry was, in contrast, spiritual, powerful and wise. It is for this reason that Paul characterises these critics as *hyperlian apostoloi*, 'exceedingly *hyper*-apostles'.

How does Paul answer these men? By what means does he justify or legitimate his ministry among the Corinthians? Five passages in 2 Corinthians show the tests Paul applied to himself.

Chapter Eight

2 CORINTHIANS

A pure gospel and changed lives

> *i. 2:17-3:2*
> For we are not, like so many, peddlers of God's word; but as men of sincerity, as commissioned by God, in the sight of God we speak in Christ. Are we beginning to commend ourselves again? Or do we need, as some do, letters of recommendation to you, or from you? You yourselves are our letter of recommendation, written on your hearts, to be known and read by all men.

Paul complains that the newcomers *peddle* the gospel, the *word of God*. The verb *kapeleuein* means to add, for example, water to pure wine, thus enabling the selling of an impure product for improper profits. Elsewhere he objects that they proclaim 'another Jesus . . . a different gospel' (11:4). Clearly he believed that these persons here altered the very message of the gospel. A major problem with John Wimber's views is that he says so little about the content of the proclamation which the 'signs and wonders' are intended to demonstrate. We read almost nothing about the actual message itself, nor do we feel exhorted and encouraged to proclaim it. All the emphasis is on the accompanying 'power' in 'signs and wonders'. But Paul wrote elsewhere that the gospel *itself* was the 'power of God for salvation' (Rom 7:16).

By contrast, Paul speaks as a man *of sincerity* (literally 'tested by the sun') and as an apostle called *by God* (near Damascus). As a consequence of his speaking the *word of God*, there had been great changes in the lives of the Corinthians. Many had been habitually immoral, idolatrous, drunken and dishonest but as now converted people they are so no more (1 Cor 6:9-11). Paul likens them to a *letter* from Christ which the world at large *reads*, a letter *delivered* ('ministered') by Paul. Unlike the intruding newcomers, Paul needs no letters commendatory from church leaders elsewhere; the Corinthians themselves in their converted lives are Christ's letter of commendation for Paul's ministry.

The radically changed lifestyle of this congregation is what legitimates Paul as a true minister of God.

Verbal and rational persuasion

ii. 5:10-13
For we must all appear before the judgment seat of Christ, so that each one may receive good or evil, according to what he has one in the body. Therefore, knowing the fear of the Lord, we persuade men; but what

> we are is known to God, and I hope it is known also to your conscience. We are not commending ourselves to you again but giving you cause to be proud of us, so that you may be able to answer those who pride themselves on a man's position and not on his heart. For if we are beside ourselves, it is for God; if we are in our right mind, it is for you.

Knowing that all must stand before the judgment seat of Christ Paul persuades men to be 'reconciled to God' (5:20). It is to this active ministry of evangelical 'persuasion' that Paul directs the attention of the Corinthians. This is why they can be proud of him and by which they can answer those who are critical of or dissatisfied with his ministry.

Paul here distinguishes between God and man. He 'persuades' men but is *known* to God. If he is *beside himself* (literally 'ecstatic') it is for God; if he is in *his right mind* (self-controlled', as demon-possessed Legion was after his encounter with Jesus) it is for men (those to whom he ministers).

In other words, Paul's ecstatic behaviour (possibly glossolalia) is between himself and God; it is not to legitimate or validate Paul's ministry to men. Two things legitimate his ministry. First, his 'persuading of men' to turn from rebellion against God to be reconciled with him. Secondly, he conducts this ministry with a 'right mind'.

It is clear that Paul was in some sense a mystical and ecstatic person. It is equally clear that he did not point to this to legitimate his ministry. What he did point to in this regard is all that anyone can point to—that he 'persuades' men, with a 'right mind', to accept reconciliation with God through the death of his Son. Paul's disavowal of the paranormal (ecstasy) on the one hand and his positive affirmation of verbal ministry on the other is eloquent testimony to the proclamatory character of apostolic ministry, one that was not dependant on 'signs and wonders'.

Effectiveness lies in dedication to God's Word, the gospel

iii. 10:3-5
For though we live in the world we are not carrying on a worldly war, for the weapons of our warfare are not worldly but have divine power to destroy strongholds. We destroy arguments and every proud obstacle to the knowledge of God, and take every thought captive to obey Christ.

Paul is here answering the charges that he is only 'weighty and strong' from a distance, by letter, and that when physically present his speech is contemptible (10:10) and his ministry weak (cf. 10:1) and *worldly* (literally 'fleshly'). That is to say, Paul's ministry is mediocre, ordinary, powerless.

Using a siege metaphor, Paul replies in the strongest terms that his weapons are powerful, with God to cast down the strongholds of arguments and high obstacles to the knowledge of God. Paul not only successfully penetrates the strong fortresses of pride and argument, he also captivates every thought and brings the man under the obedience of Christ. Through Paul's much-maligned ministry such proud, argumentative disobedience is brought captive to the obedience of Christ.

What is this ministry? There are echoes of it which may be heard throughout this letter.

1:19	The Son of God whom we *proclaimed* among you
2:14	God . . . through us spreads the fragrance of the *knowledge* of [Christ] everywhere
4:5	. . . we *proclaim* . . . Jesus Christ as Lord
4:4,6	the *gospel/knowledge* of the glory of God/Christ
5:11	we *persuade* men
5:18,19,20	God gave us and entrusted to us the *m i n i s t r y / w o r d* of reconciliation—be reconciled to God

It is quite obvious that the ministry Paul insisted was so powerfully effective was a *verbal* ministry, a ministry of the word, a gospel ministry. It is also obvious that the power of this ministry was located in the *word* spoken, not in the person of the speaker, not even in such paranormal gifts that he may possess. The *word* spoken, insofar as it is true to the apostolic gospel is, of course, not man's but *God's* Word. It is God's Word, the gospel, by analogy with Genesis 1, that brings light (4:6) and indeed nothing less than a new creation (5:11,17).

It seems to me that the reason why so many are now attracted to the paranormal, to 'signs and wonders', is that they either do not know or do not have confidence in the apostolic gospel. There is, in fact, great confusion among Christians as to what the gospel actually is. John Wimber's books do nothing to clarify this for us. He shows little interest either in defining the gospel or in promoting its proclamation.

What, then, is it that legitimates the minister in the ministry of the New Covenant? It is not his 'giftedness', nor his power, nor his paranormal actions and knowledge. Rather, it is his dedication to the word of God, a word to which he neither adds nor from which he subtracts (cf.. 4:1-3).

Weakness for the sake of others

iv. 12:7-10
And to keep me from being too elated by the abundance of revelations, a thorn was given me in the flesh, a messenger of Satan, to harass me, to

> keep me from being too elated. Three times I besought the Lord about this, that is should leave me; but he said to me, 'My grace is sufficient for you, for my power is made perfect in weakness'. I will all the more gladly boast of my weaknesses, that the power of Christ may rest upon me. For the sake of Christ, then, I am content with weaknesses, insults, hardships, persecutions, and calamaties; for when I am weak, then I am strong.

Paul does not identify his *thorn* (*skolops*). Whatever it was, it ought to be thought of not as a 'splinter' but as a 'stake'—*a stake to nail Paul to the ground after the abundance of revelations, to keep him from being too elated.* By referring to it as a 'messenger of Satan' Paul is calling to mind the afflictions of Job (see Job 1:8-2:8), which he, Paul, has suffered, through these fourteen years (12:2). By saying that the 'thorn' was given—given by God, as the divine passive indicates—Paul is making a further point of comparison between himself and Job.

There is every indication, therefore, that Paul's sufferings were God's will for him. Such a view is unacceptable to the healing theologians who insist that good health is the birthright of every believer in consequence of Christ's atoning death (see *Power Healing*, 164-171). Yet Paul prayed *three times* for the removal of the 'thorn', and it remained. Jesus prayed twice that the cup would be taken from him, but it was not (Mark 14:32-42). It is not always God's purpose to relieve us of suffering. Some claim that Paul's was a special case, but there is no evidence that it was.

In response to his prayer the Lord said (the Greek perfect *eireken* indicating that Paul still heard him, despite the passing of many years):

> My grace is sufficient for you
> my power is made perfect in weakness
> (12:9).

By 'weakness' Paul means not only the 'thorn' but also the *weaknesses, hardships, persecutions and calamities* which have accompanied his apostolic ministry. It must not pass unnoticed that this letter, which is *par excellence* his defence of his legitimacy in ministry, is the letter in which he lists on no less than four occasions his catalogue of weakness and suffering (4:7-12; 6:1-10; 11:23-33; 12:7-10). The sufferings of Jesus, by which he saved humanity, flow on into history in the lives of ministers of the gospel as they 'persuade' men and women to 'be reconciled to God'. In this vein Paul wrote:

> Death is at work in us,
> but life is at work in you (4:12).

The principle of suffering for the sake of others, which lay at the heart of Jesus' reconciling death, continues in the experience of apostles, missionaries and ministers.

We hear little of this today. Why? The answer is that ours is an era preoccupied with power—military power, technological power, economic power. The very book titles *Power Evangelism* and *Power Healing* reflect and are an appeal to secular, even worldly, love of power.

Like Paul's opponents, then, it is very easy today to believe that God's power is perfected in our power—*power in power*. Our longing for 'signs and wonders', for the display of power in our midst, is little different from the worldly pursuit of power so evident in the lives of many politicians and entrepeneurs. It is an ungodly ego, however, that desires to control and manipulate people and events. To such people, pagan or Christian, Paul's words come as a shocking rebuke: 'Christ's power is made perfect *in weakness*'. This is not, please note, 'special' weakness, 'contrived' weakness or 'religious' weakness, arising out of self-emptying, fasting or other spiritual exercises undertaken with a view to being 'filled'. It is the ordinary weakness of body and mind of fatigue and ageing which occurs in the lives of those who faithfully pursue the work of ministry.

Paul does not specifically call such 'weakness' a 'sign' of the gospel, but that in truth is what it is, as the fourfold list of apostolic sufferings in this letter makes clear. It is our great problem today that few of us, including those who don't accept Mr. Wimber's teaching, are prepared to accept what Paul says, so contrary is it to the spirit of the age. For most of us Paul's lesson is still to be learned!

Signs and the true apostolic period

> *v. 12:11-12*
> I have been a fool! You forced me to it, for I ought to have been commended by you. For I am not at all inferior to these superlative apostles, even though I am nothing. The signs of a true apostle were performed among you in all patience, with signs and wonders and mighty works.

The *superlative apostles* (*hyperlian apostoloi*, cf.. 11:5) are probably to be identified with the 'false apostles' referred to earlier (11:15). These are different ways of referring to the same judaising group recently arrived in Corinth. Paul coined the word *hyperlian* ('superlative') to show up their self-declared superiority. Their key word was *hyper*, which means 'above', 'over' or 'better'. Paul writes of their missionary triumphalism as '*over*-extending themselves' (10:14, *hyperekteinein*) into 'lands *beyond*' (10:16, *ta hyperekeina*). Paul's ironic self-references expose their '*abundance* of

Paul, the Miraculous and Ministry

revelations' (12:7, *te hyperbole ton apokalypseon*) and *super*-elation (12:7, *hyperairesthai*).

Clearly they present themselves as sufficient, powerful, wise, spiritual and triumphant, whereas Paul was portrayed as inadequate, weak, a fool, worldly and defeated. So, far from rebutting these criticisms, Paul has written at some length about his foolishness and weakness to show how wrong-headed his opponents' claim for legitimacy based on 'power' really is. Paul has spoken about his weaknesses at such length (11:22-12:10) precisely because Christ's power is perfected not in power, as they say it is, but in *weakness*.

Nonetheless, Paul does not concede the inferiority to these newcomers which they claim. The signs of an apostle were indeed performed among the Corinthians (the divine passive 'performed' indicating that these 'signs' were wrought *by God)*. These *hyper*-apostles sought to legitimate their ministry by visions, revelations and ecstatic speech. Did they also point to *signs, wonders and mighty works*? Quite possibly they did in fact seek to perform miraculous works. Palestine, from which they came, was experiencing an intensive period of attempted sign-working, associated with self-styled prophets like Theudas and the Egyptian. Theudas tried to make the Jordan part; the Egyptian sought to command the walls of Jerusalem to collapse. Others attempted to perform 'signs of freedom and salvation' in the wilderness. It is quite conceivable that the *hyper*-apostles from

Palestine sought to legitimate their ministry by miraculous phenomena.

There were many who denied that Paul was an apostle, in particular the judaisers who rejected both his doctrines and his apostolic claims. He, however, frequently reiterated his claims that he was truly an apostle of Christ.

Gal 1:1	Paul an apostle—not from men or through men—but through Jesus Christ
Gal 1:15-16	God . . . revealed his Son to me . . . that I . . . preach him among the Gentiles
Gal 2:8	[God] who worked through Peter for the apostolate to the circumcised worked through me also for [the apostolate] to the Gentiles
1 Cor 9:1	Am I not an apostle? Have I not seen Jesus our Lord?
1 Cor 15:6-11	He appeared . . . to all the apostles . . . to me . . . the least of the apostles
2 Cor 1:1	Paul . . . an apostle of Christ Jesus through the will of God
2 Cor 10:8; 13:10	our authority (*exousia*) which the Lord gave for building you up (i.e. the Gentiles).

It is clear from the Acts of the Apostles and from Romans that Paul performed the miracle signs which attested the other apostles. The Acts describes:

13:4-12	the temporary blindness of Bar-Jesus in Salamis
14:1-7	the granting of 'signs and wonders' in Iconium
14:8-10	the healing of the cripple in Lystra
16:16-18	the expulsion of the Spirit of divination from the girl in Philippi
19:14	exorcisms in Ephesus
20:9-10	the raising(?) of Eutyches in Troas
28:3	the survival of Paul from snakebite in Malta

It is apparent that Paul showed by these 'signs and wonders' that he was no less an apostle than others before him who also performed 'signs and wonders'.

In the letter to the Romans, Paul is diplomatically preparing the Roman Christians for his pending visit to them. He assured them that he was only 'passing' through (to Spain, 15:24) and that he would not remain with them. That would be to 'build on another man's foundation' (15:20). This is almost certainly a reference to Peter, who had probably by that time settled in Rome as leader of the Jewish Christians there as an apostle to the circumcision. It will be remembered that Paul (and Barnabas) had agreed with Peter (and James and John) that they should go to Gentiles and Jews respectively and that neither should trespass into the other's sphere of apostolic ministry (Gal 2:7-9). It is for this reason Paul will only pass through Rome and not stay there.

There were judaisers soon afterward in Rome (see Phil 1:15-18), and it is reasonable to assume that they and their anti-Paul attitudes were present in Rome in the middle to late fifties when he wrote the letter to the Romans. It was necessary, therefore, for Paul to establish with these people that he was, truly, the apostle to the Gentiles. Accordingly, he makes the explicit claim to be the apostle to the Gentiles (Rom 1:5-6; 15:15-16; 16:25-26), stating further:

> I will not venture to speaking of anything except what Christ has wrought through me to win obedience from the Gentiles, by word and deed, by the power of signs and wonders, by the power of the Holy Spirit, so that from Jerusalem as far round as Illyricum I have fully preached the gospel of Christ (15:18-20).

In other words, Paul has demonstrated his unique apostleship both by evangelising Gentiles in the circle from Jerusalem to Illyricum *and* by performing apostolic signs and wonders. By these descriptions he establishes, in defence to his judaising detractors, that he is in every sense of the word, an apostle of Christ.

It is clear that the apostolic office was special, limited to a small group of persons, whose singular

Paul, the Miraculous and Ministry

ministry was demonstrated by 'signs and wonders'. Apostles were raised up in the first generation of the new faith both to provide missionary leadership and, also, within that context, to preach and write the authentic gospel of Christ. The Spirit worked in apostles as receptors and transmitters of the revelation of God in Christ (Rom 16:25-26; Eph 3:1-5; 1 Cor 2:1-13).

Since Christ was God's full and final revelation to humanity and since apostles authenticated that revelation, it follows that apostles do not continue beyond the entry of Christ into history. Christ, revelation and apostles belong clustered together within the one great epoch, to which the New Testament bears witness and from which the apostolic writings arose. To imply 'signs and wonders' continue into history is to infer that apostles, and therefore revelation, continue into history. But that, clearly, would be to diminish Christ's unique person and work. Therefore, the 'signs and wonders' as spoken of by John Wimber have no place in history beyond the apostolic generation.

What, then, are we to make of miraculous phenomena which periodically occur? What are we to think of John Wimber himself, in particular the 'words of knowledge' to which he lays claim?

Chapter Nine

MIRACLES AND MINISTRY TODAY

Since God is above and beyond the perceived natural order, we should be open to the possibility of God answering our prayers in supranatural ways. There is, however, a difference between being 'open' to God so acting and 'expecting' him to do so. Is not to 'expect' him so to act the same as demanding that he act in that way? Have we not trespassed on to 'holy ground' where we as sinful mortals have no right to be?

There is no reason, however, why the 'spiritual gifts' as mentioned by Paul in 1 Corinthians 12, some of which appear miraculous in character, should not continue into history down to our own day. These do not appear to be associated with evangelism and missionary work so much as within the corporate life of the Christian community.

If John Wimber gives expression to 'words of knowledge' in the way that he claims, we should, I think, regard him as a Christian mystic. As such, he is but one of the many mystics within Judaism and Christianity, and indeed outside those faiths, who appear to have had paranormal powers. The rabbi Hanina ben Dosa, who lived a few decades after Jesus, knew when his prayers for healing would be effective. He 'knew' that the sick for whom he prayed would be healed 'whenever the prayer was fluent in his mouth'. In the end, however, such mystic power proves nothing, since many non-Christians have enjoyed these gifts.

Certainly, for Paul in 2 Corinthians, visions, revelations and ecstatic speech were neither here nor there in relationship to the ministry of the New Covenant. What really mattered in the recognition and legitimation of ministry was that there were converted people whose changed lives spoke volumes about the ministry to the watching world. The thing that Corinthians and all congregations can take pride in is that those who minister to them are not mystics, but that they faithfully seek to *persuade* men to be reconciled to God. Against the put-down that his verbal ministry is mundane, weak and powerless, Paul replies that the gospel is divinely empowered to capture the proud and fortified ego for its obedience to Christ. In contrast to those who declare power to be perfected in power, Paul points not to his spectacular visions but to the sufferings of the thorn and the weakness engendered by faithful apostolic ministry. Finally, he will say in all humility that he is not less than the *hyper*-apostles but that the signs of the apostles—signs which other apostles have performed in demonstration of their genuineness—these signs Paul has also performed. As for those who deny to him the apostleship to the Gentiles, with all that is implied about his Christ-given authority to teach the Gentiles, let them know that as other apostles have performed 'signs and wonders', so too has he. But there is no reason to expect such 'signs and wonders' to continue into history for the very good reason that we do not

Paul, the Miraculous and Ministry

expect revelation to continue into history. Christ came once for all (*hapax*), bringing once for all the full revelation of God to men in salvation. That revelation was made to the apostles and through them. They belong to the era of Christ, and only then; so, too, do 'signs and wonders'.

Part Three

HISTORICAL PERSPECTIVE

by

John Reid

Chapter Ten

THE GREAT EVANGELICAL AWAKENING

I commence this historical perspective by quoting two texts of Scripture:

Jer 5:24   Let us fear the Lord our God who gives autumn and spring rains in season . . .

Joel 2:23   for He has given you a teacher of righteousness. He sends you abundant showers, both autumn and spring rains as before.

These are two favourite texts of many people in the broad Pentecostal movement when they discuss signs and wonders. Their exegesis is that the first rains (autumn) represent the apostolic ministry when the first fruits of evangelism were brought in with power. The second rains (spring) will lead to the great harvest immediately before the second coming of Christ. Frank Bartleman, in *As It Was in the Beginning*, writes:

> But here we are with the restoration of the very experience of Pentecost with the latter rain—a restoration of power to finish up the work begun. We shall again be lifted up to the Church's former level, to complete her work,

> begin where they left off when failure
> overtook them and speedily fulfilling
> the last great commission and open the
> way for the coming of Christ.[1]

Consequently, the remarkable growth of Pentecostalism and the so-called discovery of signs and wonders is said by many to be God's last act before the end. The point of this section is to ask whether these phenomena have appeared since the apostles, and how our forbears have handled the matter.

In AD156 the movement called Montanism appeared in the early church. Professor J S Whale comments that 'Montanism is the classic example of a sect-type destined to appear constantly in the history of the Church from that day to this'.[2]

Reinbold Seeberg in his *Text Book of Doctrines* pointed out the striking similarity at almost every point between Montanism and Pentecostalism.[3] Both anticipated that the last period of God's dealings with men and women had come with the discovery of God's gifts, and both movements stressed the centrality of the paraclete.

It would be possible to look at signs and wonders at various stages of church history. For instance, Tertullian placed a very high value on exorcism in apologetics and evangelism. But I want to come much nearer to our own time and to look at our own evangelical tradition. We are heirs to the great evangelical awakening of the eighteenth century in the United Kingdom. Of course that awakening was very widespread and profoundly affected the American colonies, Europe and especially Norway. Both Bishop J C Ryle and Archbishop M L Loane have written about Anglican leaders who were caught up in that time of renewal. Ryle wrote of the remarkable signs of spiritual power which occurred when John Berridge of Everton preached:

> It is undeniable that in a certain period of Berridge's ministry very curious physical effects were produced on those who were aroused by his preaching. Some of his hearers cried out hysterically, some were thrown into strong convulsions and some fell into a kind of trance or catalepsy which lasted a long time.[4]

Bishop Ryle wryly commented that it was all mysterious and 'a minister ought certainly not to be put down as a fanatic because people go into convulsions under his preaching'.[5] In *Cambridge and the Evangelical Succession,* Archbishop Loane writes of extraordinary demonstrations of spiritual phenomena. People fell down in church with such suddenness that pews were smashed. It was recorded that there were times when people, after leaving church, would drop on the road or on their way home. 'They would fall down like dead men or lie where they fell on the road or in the garden'. The archbishop comments, 'We need not now feel concerned either to defend or explain these things; they passed away in the course of time but they were a sign to many that God was there in power both to wound and to heal.'[6]

John Wesley

I make brief mention of three great figures in the Revival. The first one was the remarkable and outstanding evangelist, John Wesley. Wesley actually encouraged the manifestations of what we called signs and wonders. He would stop preaching and go into the crowd to minister to those who were displaying unusual activity. This extract from his journal of May 2, 1739, when he was in Bristol, could have been written yesterday by someone involved in a so-called Pentecostal evangelistic service:

> John Haydon . . . a man of regular life and conversation . . . changed colour, fell off his chair and began screaming terribly and beating himself upon the ground . . . Two or three men were holding him as well as they could. He immediately fixed his eyes on me and cried, 'Aye, this is he who I said was a deceiver of all the people but God has overtaken me. I said it was all a delusion'. He then roared out, 'O thou devil! Thou cursed devil, yea thou legions of

> devils, thou canst not stay'. He then
> beat himself upon the ground again,
> his breast heaving at the same time as
> in the pangs of death and great drops
> of sweat trickling down his face. We
> all took ourselves to prayer. His
> pangs ceased and both body and soul
> were set at liberty.[7]

This kind of activity was common, and there were often healings, exorcisms, slaying in the spirit, and so forth. The evangelical expression to describe these activities was being 'cut to the heart by the sword of the Spirit'. While Wesley was an active promoter of signs and wonders in evangelism, he was later somewhat wistfully to write, 'But although they saw "signs and wonders" (for so I term them), yet many would not believe'.[8]

George Whitefield

George Whitefield was the evangelist without a peer. But just as John Wesley encouraged so-called signs and wonders, George Whitefield discouraged them. In fact, he went further than discouraging them. He rebuked people in his congregations who started to show signs of unusual or abnormal activity. He wrote to Wesley on the subject:

> I cannot think it right for you to give
> so much encouragement to those
> convulsions which people have been

> thrown into under your ministry. Were I to do so, how many more would cry out every night. I think it is tempting God to require such signs. That there is something of God in it I doubt not, but the devil, I believe, does impose. I think it will encourage the French prophets, take people from the written word and make them depend on visions, convulsions, etc., more than the promise and precepts of the gospel.[9]

The reactions to signs and wonders was varied. Some like Wesley encouraged it. Some saw him as the divinely appointed channel for this purpose. In his biography of George Whitefield, Dallimore conjectures that as signs and wonders passed away in Wesley's ministry, he turned to give prominence to a second experience of grace in the process of Christian initiation.[10] Although he did not discount signs and wonders out of hand, Whitefield actively discouraged their manifestation. Finally, there were some who were thoroughly opposed. They saw the phenomena as a distraction which reduced gospel preaching to emotionalism.

Jonathan Edwards

Jonathan Edwards stands as the third central figure in the Great Evangelical Awakening. Edwards ministered in a church in Northampton, New

Historical Perspective

England, in the eighteenth century. He was later a missionary to Indians, and finally president of the college which was to become Princeton. He is today regarded as the greatest intellectual figure of the eighteenth century in America, and was distinguished both as a philosopher and as a theologian. About 1740 a remarkable revival broke out in New England, and Edwards was a supporter and a leader of it. He managed to get Whitefield to come, and there are remarkable descriptions of the crowds descending on Northampton to hear the great evangelist.

The revival in New England was similar to the revival in the United Kingdom. When Edwards preached, 'several stout men fell as though a cannon had been discharged and a ball had made its way through their hearts'. The response to the revival was varied. There were determined attacks upon it which centred on the new style of evangelistic preaching, the emphasis on new birth and assurance, the Calvinistic theology of many of the leaders of the revival, and there was certainly opposition to what Edwards admits were 'irregularities and imprudencies'. It was because of the complexity of the issues that Edwards wrote in 1741 his book *The Distinguishing Marks of a Word of the Spirit of God*. It was both a defence of the revival and a critique of its preoccupation with the abnormal.

The work consisted of sixty-one pages. The first section of the book deals with the position that it was not unnatural to expect unusual happenings where the Holy Spirit is active. 'I do not know that we have any express mention in the New Testament of any person's weeping or groaning or sighing through fear of hell or a sense of God's anger; but is there anybody so foolish as from hence to argue that in whomsoever these things appear, their convictions are not from the Spirit of God.'[11] He defended those who out of desperate conviction or joyous enthusiasm 'make a great deal of noise about religion'.[12] He did not see that a work of God should be condemned because of imprudencies or irregularities. 'It is no wonder that in a mixed multitude of all sorts .. there are many who behave themselves imprudently.'[13] He goes further. Even if some fall into gross errors or scandalous practices, that was no argument that the work in general was not the work of the Spirit of God.

In the second section, he gave five distinguishing evidences of a work of God:

1. When the operation is such to raise esteem of that Jesus who was born of the Virgin and was crucified without the gate of Jerusalem . . . establish the truth . . . of his being the Son of God and the Saviour of men; it is a sure sign that it is from the Spirit of God.[14]
2. When the Spirit that is at work operates against the interests of Satan's kingdom which lies in encouraging and establishing sin . . . this is a sure sign that it is from the Spirit of God.[15]

3. The Spirit that operates in such a manner as to cause in men a great regard to the Holy Scriptures and establish them more in their truth and divinity is certainly the Spirit of God.[16]
4. The Spirit . . . operates as spirit of truth, leading persons to truth, convincing them of those things which are true.[17]
5. The Spirit that is at work among a people operates as a Spirit of love to God and man, it is a sure sign that it is the Spirit of God.[18]

He stated that it is impossible for the devil to give these convictions because 'he cannot give those things he has not himself'.[19]

Section two of the book is a practical exploration of the principles underlying the revival in New England. He had no doubt 'that the extraordinary influence that lately has appeared causing an uncommon concern and engagedness of mind about the things of religion is undoubtedly, in the general, from the Spirit of God'.[20] He himself had been witness 'for some months past' to people crying out, great agonies of body, and the like.[21] Evidently, these phenomena had raised the charge that such confusion could not come from God. Edwards rebutted this. These were people being liberated, and so he wrote, 'Would to God that all the public assemblies in the land were broken off from their public exercises with such confusions as this the next Sabbath day'.[22] Having defended the revival and pleaded with people not to oppose it, Edwards distinguished the extraordinary gifts of the Spirit from the graces of the Spirit. The graces of the Spirit are the glorious operations of the Spirit and more excellent than the extraordinary and the miraculous. For this he depended on 1 Corinthians 12:31ff.

Graces of the Spirit

In a fine passage Edwards wrote:

> It was not the gifts but the graces of the apostles that was to proper evidence of their names being written in heaven; in which Christ directs them to rejoice, much more than in the devil's being subject to them. To have grace in the heart is a higher privilege than the blessed Virgin herself had in having the body of the second person of the Trinity conceived in her womb, by the power of the Highest overshadowing her: Luke 11:27,28. [23]

Edwards estimated that the extraordinary gifts of the Spirit, on the basis of St Paul's First Epistle to the Corinthians, are childish in comparison to the Spirit's operation in giving love. Because in 1 Corinthians it is said that the spectacular and extraordinary gifts will fail, cease and vanish, he wrote, 'I do not expect a restoration of these miraculous gifts in the approaching glorious times of the Church, nor do I desire it . . . . For my own part, I had rather enjoy the sweet influence of the Spirit, showing Christ's spiritual divine beauty, infinite grace and dying love drawing forth the holy exercises of faith, divine love, sweet complaisance and humble joy in God, one quarter of an hour than to have prophetic visions and revelations the whole year'.[24] Again, 'It does not appear to me that there is any need of those extraordinary gifts to introduce this happy state and set up the Kingdom of God throughout the world; I have seen so much of the power of God in a more excellent way as to convince me that God can easily do without it'.[25]

Edwards is an important witness. He was a theologian and pastor of the first rank. He was an enthusiastic supporter of the revival and sensitive to those who had overwhelming emotional and physical experiences. He wrote both as a witness, pastor and theologian. He saw the sign and wonder which is the enduring witness to the power of the gospel in the proud man or woman who was transformed by the love of Christ.

Reflections on the present

What reflections can we make on the view that signs and wonders are the signs of the latter rain and that all authentic evangelism will be preceded, accompanied or followed by some sign of spiritual power?

First of all, we can categorically reject any notion that these things have not occurred before. It is a mistake to see these as the unique forerunners of the Second Coming.

Secondly, we should not be surprised to see the ambivalence of the New Testament on signs and wonders reflected in the church's life. When Jesus was tempted at the beginning of his ministry, Satan urged him to jump off the temple tower. In refusing to respond to this temptation, he showed that the kingdom was not to be established by the exercise of miracles and wonders. Nevertheless, they did occur significantly in his ministry, and despite the remarkable signs he effected, very few believed in him. In fact, Jesus saw that the response of many to his signs and wonders was a hunger for the abnormal and sensational, and for this they were rebuked. It was this very thing which concerned George Whitefield, for he saw it lead people away from the promises of God's Word.

Thirdly, we cannot fail to see that signs and wonders can be supplied or prevented by the attitude of the evangelist. This is the significance of the Wesley-Whitefield interaction. Strong personalities and powerful preaching can create the climate when the abnormal is encouraged.

Fourthly, Edwards saw that even when signs and wonders occur, they must not be given a place beyond their importance, for they are at the periphery of evangelism. He was to write, 'A work is not to be judged by an effects on the bodies of men such as tears, groans, tumbling, loud cries, agonies of body or the failing of bodily strength'. What endures is the preaching of the Cross. This message does not need additives to give it more power.

Finally, the evangelical revival shows the danger of pursuing spiritual power in terms of the spectacular. The signs and wonders were to pass after a few years. But what has to be grasped is that powerlessness has an extraordinary dynamic in God's affairs. The world cannot recognise it. But when Christ was abandoned to powerlessness by man and God ('He cannot save himself', said a bystander), the power of redemption and transformation became apparent. In fact, there has never been any power comparable to the power of Christ crucified. The pursuit of signs and wonders can become worldly if it obscures the fact that by dying we live, by becoming poor we are enriched, and by being made helpless we become strong.

Conclusion

THINKING THROUGH THE IMPLICATIONS

by

Robert Doyle

Chapter Eleven

OUR EXPERIENCE OF GOD

At least three criticisms of contemporary evangelical Christianity emerge from John Wimber's ministry. The first is that it has become a religion of the mind only. The second is that it involves belief in a God who acted in the past, will act in the future, but does not act today. The third is that what God is expected to do today is only what we programme for.

Wimber's antidote to these things poses difficult questions. The imperative to pursue 'power evangelism' and embrace the 'transrational' middle ground between the rational and the supernatural drives us back to Holy Scripture. Do we really understand the religion of the Bible? Or are we somehow, because of tradition, temperament, or just plain ignorance, off centre?

This concluding chapter seeks to draw some of the major threads together, focus central questions, and offer a way forward.

Expectations

Religious behaviour is very much determined by our view of God and and how we meet him. The confrontation between Elijah and the prophets of Baal in 1 Kings 18 is a case in point. Baal, the cruel, remote and orgiastic god is met in blood, fatigue and ecstasy, as verses 26-29 highlight.

Yahweh, the God of Abraham, Isaac and Israel, the God of word and promise, is met with faith, simple prayer and obedience (vv. 36-37). What God is like shapes our expectations of how we will meet him.

What does the behaviour of a 'signs and wonders' meeting indicate? It is not a 'Baal' occasion. John Wimber is a consummate leader. Clear directions and comments honestly seek to acknowledge the differing operations of individuals' emotions, crowd effects and the presence of the Spirit working. The lead-up by song and teaching and exhortation, and the results in the time of ministry point to an orthodox view of God and a modified view of meeting him. John Wimber certainly expects to meet God in his Word, but the direction and content of his gatherings seem to point, and without apology, to a greater practical concern. God is expected to be encountered in phenomena, the 'supernatural', and in emotional ecstasy.

The signs and wonders movement expects to meet God in Word and event, to be responded to with faith, and emotional and physical effects.

But this is not the expectation towards which the Bible's promises and commands direct us. God is encountered in his Word. The expected response is faith. This is because God is a person, not a force.

The Bible is not just a collection of revealed truths. When we encounter the Word enscriptured we encounter God. This is plain from the earliest statements about Scripture (Deut 28-31;

Josh 1:8-9) and the place of Scripture in Jesus' teaching (see Matt 22:31), as well as the rest of the New Testament (see Heb 3:7).

God promises and commands us to meet him in Holy Scripture, and he calls forth from us the response of faith. There are no such promises or commands for contemporary emotional and physical events and their appropriate response. A careful study of context will not support an expectation to meet God in silence, for example. The pattern in the meditative Psalms is instructive. In dire straits the writer seeks to meet God. He works out his despondency by remembering the mighty works and promises of God in the history of creation and salvation, and responds with faith, trust.

> My spirit faints within me; my heart within me is appalled.
> I remember the days of old, I meditate on all that thou hast done;
> I muse on what thy hands have wrought . . .
> Let me hear in the morning of thy steadfast love,
> for in thee I put my trust (Ps 143:4-8).

Faith, created by the gospel word, is *the* experience of the Christian life. And what does faith look like? The New Testament has a very full description of the life of faith. It is the life of relationship with God: trust and obedience, love of

God and love of neighbour, godliness, the relational fruits of the Spirit (Gal 5:16-26).

Now John Wimber may have no quarrel with all this, but his teachings point to more than enscriptured Word and present faith as mature Christian experience of God. Because there is no biblical promise or command for a contemporary 'word of knowledge' and 'divine appointments', Wimber's message is a serious challenge to the sufficiency of Scripture, to the Bible alone. It is Holy Scripture's own self-testimony that it is sufficient for the complete Christian life (2 Tim 3:15-17). 'Bible alone' as an evangelical distinctive was hammered out in the Reformation century against the Roman Catholics who insisted that God also spoke a contemporary word through the church, and the radical Anabaptists who saw the same extra word coming through the inspired individual. Both groups taught that the Christian life was incomplete without this word and structured their religious behaviour accordingly.

We live in a time when, as even casual scanning of the TV program shows, there is tremendous, and credulous interest in the miraculous. In this context we need to look very hard at people's perceptions of signs and wonders when they are presented in worship services. It is all too easy to claim that they only enhance people's grasp of the simple gospel of forgiveness. But do they? Or do they make this gospel somehow only a preliminary, rather dull background to the 'real action'? Clark H Pinnock's remarks in *Christianity Today* (August 8, 1986, p. 19) bear consideration:

> Furthermore, the masses are easily excited by charismania, by an overemphasis on the spectacular, to the detriment of the ongoing works of charity. A generation whipped up to a frenzy by high-tech show biz may well demand charismatic Christianity and be bored with anything else. But we must be careful not to tailor our presentation entirely to market requirements.

The expectation [*"Expectations"*] of meeting God in his Word has long been nurtured in Protestant worship by Bible readings, saying of Psalms, sermon outlines and the like. Similarly, in a signs and wonders meeting, expectations of the supernatural and the affective are nurtured by continuous chorus singing and exhortations to joy and expectancy. The expectations, and hence the activities of the signs and wonders movement, are deficient because they are formed outside of the promises of biblical revelation. Our disagreement with Wimber is not based on personal preferences for cerebral over emotional activity, but on the promises of God. However we must also subject our own patterns of behaviour to careful scrutiny.

A new shape for evangelical ministry?

Perhaps one reason for the attraction of the signs and wonders model of ministry is that Historical Protestantism is diminishing in its ability to win and hold converts to Jesus Christ.

The statistics are discouraging. The results from the McNair Anderson poll of 1983/84 and the Australian Values Studies Survey carried out by the Roy Morgan Research Centre in 1983 show that on a national basis 21 per cent of Australians attend church weekly. Among the 26 per cent of Australians who are nominally Anglican, 9 per cent of them attend church weekly. Similar proportions apply to other denominations of Historical Protestantism.[1]

The situation is no better in the uniquely evangelical Anglican diocese of Sydney. In 1986, along with several other denominations, special survey forms were completed by church attenders. On census Sunday only 1.9 per cent of Australians, or 7.6 per cent of nominal Anglicans, chose to be in church in evangelical Sydney.[2] As 83 per cent of those surveyed attended weekly, it suggests that a very small pool of nominal Anglicans visit their church more than yearly; or to put it another way, perhaps 90 per cent of Anglicans have only infrequent contact with their church, if any.

Against this background, the programme offered by John Wimber looks successful, and attractive. However, the argument of this book is that it is an unacceptable alternative because of wrong expectations and emphases. It is also unacceptable because it diverts evangelicals from addressing the real problems associated with effective evangelism and church life. The reasons for numerical decline are complex, but some are all too evident.

Within Australian Anglicanism, an evangelical faces a constant tension between denominational pressure to maintain high profile sixteenth and nineteenth-century customs, like antiquated dress and the small parish system, and the apostle's example of becoming 'all things to all men that I might by all means save some' (1 Cor 9:22). To most of the sub-cultures that make up modern society, our ways are unintelligible. They hide the real Christ. Even our best liturgical efforts are complex in their sentence structure and use. First Order Holy Communion in *An Australian Prayer Book* (1978) has been assessed against the norms of the Plain English movement pioneered by Professor Eagleson of the University of Sydney and Kath White of the Adult Literacy Office. Based on the sentence and word length, the reader needs at least thirteen years of education.[3] If church is unintelligible, it will be boring, and few will come (still fewer will stay) to discover what it is all about.

Theological educators must take responsibility here. Ministers must be trained to critically appreciate the function and communication of Christianity in our surrounding culture.

Faced with the enormity of the challenge, one reaction is a conservatism which we know will be applauded by at least some church members and colleagues. Another is to uncritically and desperately jump on the nearest passing bandwagon. Of course, this is overstatement! But, if we identify even partly with the description, then the apostle Paul has the solution, as his concerns in 2 Corinthians amply demonstrate. 'So we do not lose heart . . . for the things which are seen are transient, but the things that are unseen are eternal' (4:16).

END NOTES

EVANGELICAL MINISTRY - John Woodhouse

1. John Wimber, *Power Evangelism: Signs and Wonders Today* (London, Sydney, Auckland and Toronto: Hodder and Stoughton, 1985), and *Power Healing* (London, Sydney, Auckland and Toronto: Hodder and Stoughton, 1986).
2. I am grateful to many friends who have discussed aspects of this paper with me before, during and after John Wimber's visit to Canberra in November, 1987, especially those who disagree with what I have written.
3. See chapter 1 of *Power Evangelism* for Wimber's account of this central concept in his theology.
4. *Power Evangelism*, 27.
5. See *Power Evangelism*, 25-26.
6. *Power Evangelism*, 29.
7. *Power Evangelism*, 29, cited from C Peter Wagner.
8. *Power Healing*, 204.
9. *Power Evangelism*, 47.
10. *Power Evangelism*, 56.
11. *Power Evangelism*, 56-57.
12. *Power Evangelism*, 57.
13. *Power Evangelism*, 59.
14. The main terms are *'oth* 'sign', *mopheth* 'wonder' in Hebrew, and *semeion* 'sign', *teras* 'wonder' in Greek.
15. See also Exod 3:20; 8:23; 10:1; 11:9, 10; Num 14:22; Josh 3:5
16. See also Deut 6:22; 7:19; 29:3; 34:11; Exod 15:11.

17. See also Exod 10:2.
18. See also Josh 24:17; Neh 9:10; Ps 105:27; Jer 32:21.
19. See Jer 32:20 where 'signs and wonders to this day' refers to God's judgments on the people (vv. 23-24).
20. See also Deut 26:8.
21. See also Ps 105:5 and the references in note 18.
22. See also Ps 78:42-43; 106:7; Neh 9:17.
23. See also Matt 16:1-4; 24:3-5; Mark 8:11-12; 13:4-6; Luke 11:16, 29; 21:7-8.
24. See John 2:18; 4:48; 6:30.
25. See 1 Cor 1:17-18; 15:3-5.
26. For an example of a false prophet see Hananiah in Jer 28.
27. Likewise Ezekiel performed ordinary enough acts that were called 'wonders.' See especially Ezek 12:1-11; 24:15-27.
28. 'In all patience' may suggest that Paul has in mind here something rather different from the 'signs and wonders and mighty works' claimed by his opponents at Corinth.
29. 'Thy servants' in verse 29 refers to the apostles. F F Bruce reasonably assumes that 'their friends' in verse 23 are the other apostles. F F Bruce, *The Acts of the Apostles*, NICNT (Grand Rapids: Eerdmans, 1954), 105.
30. *Power Evangelism*, 178.
31. *Power Evangelism*, 20.
32. *Power Evangelism*, 24.
33. *Power Evangelism*, 30-31.
34. *Power Evangelism*, 56-57.
35. *Power Evangelism*, 35.
36. *Power Evangelism*, 51.

37. *Power Evangelism*, 38.
38. *Power Healing*, 194-5.
39. These groups are also said to share the gospel. *Power Healing*, 198.
40. *Power Healing*, 70.
41. *Power Evangelism*, 57
42. *Power Evangelism*, 59.
43. *Power Healing*, 186.
44. *Power Healing*, 195.
45. See Exod 29:35; Deut 1:3, 41; 7:11; 12:11, 14.
46. For an appropriate example see Exod 4:1-9.
47. Lewis B Smedes, *Ministry and the Miraculous: A Case Study at Fuller Theological Seminary* (Pasadena: Fuller Theological Seminary, 1987), 30.
48. Leon Morris, *Commentary on the Gospel of John* (Grand Rapids, Michigan: Eerdmans, 1971), 691.
49. *Power Evangelism*, 49.
50. *Power Evangelism*, 50-51.
51. *Power Evangelism*, 53.
52. See, for example, *Power Evangelism*, 59 '. . . the presence of the Messiah—the embodiment of the kingdom of God—was demonstrated in *power encounters* [emphasis mine].
53. *Power Evangelism*, 60.
54. *Power Evangelism*, 43.
55. Wimber says that here Paul 'instructs them to expect power encounters' (*Power Evangelism*, 39).
56. *Power Evangelism*, 39.
57. Emphasis Wimber's. However the word translated *'few'* (following NIV) is usually translated 'some' (RSV, NASB, NEB) and means

'an indefinite quantity that is nevertheless not without importance'. However it is translated, there is no hint in the text of Acts 17 that Paul's preaching at Athens was in any sense inadequate.

58. *Power Evangelism*, 60.
59. *Power Evangelism*, 141.
60. Luke 11:9 possibly means this, but not in Wimber's terms.
61. *Power Evangelism*, 140.
62. *Power Evangelism*, 55.
63. *Power Evangelism*, 143.
64. *Power Evangelism*, 15.
65. *Power Evangelism*, 24.

HISTORICAL PERSPECTIVE - John Reid

1. F Bartleman, *How Pentecost came to Los Angeles : As It Was in the Beginning* 2nd ed. (Los Angeles: Privately printed, 1925), 88. [cited from F D Bruner, *A Theology of the Holy Spirit*, Grand Rapids: Eerdmans, 1972, 28].
2. J S Whale, *The Protestant Tradition* (Cambridge: University Press, 1955), 209.
3. Rhinold Seeberg, *Text Book of the History of Doctrine* (Grand Rapids: Baker Book House, 1956), 105-6.
4. J C Ryle, *Christian Leaders of the 18th Century* (Edinburgh: Banner of Truth, 1978), 228.
5. *Christian Leaders*, 229.
6. M L Loane, *Cambridge and the Evangelical Succession* (London: Lutterworth Press, 1952), 78.
7. N Curnock (ed), *The Journal of John Wesley* (London: Epworth, 1938), vol 2.190-191.

8. *The Journal of John Wesley*, 2.202 May 20th, 1739 [quoted Dallimore 320].
9. Cited from A A Dallimore, *George Whitefield* (London: Banner of Truth, 1970), vol 1.328.
10. *George Whitefield*, 331.
11. C C Goen (ed), *The Works of Jonathan Edwards* (New Haven: Yale University Press, 1972), vol 4.243.
12. *Works of Jonathan Edwards*, 4.234.
13. *Works of Jonathan Edwards*, 4.241.
14. *Works of Jonathan Edwards*, 4.249.
15. *Works of Jonathan Edwards*, 4.250-1.
16. *Works of Jonathan Edwards*, 4.253.
17. *Works of Jonathan Edwards*, 4.254.
18. *Works of Jonathan Edwards*, 4.254.
19. *Works of Jonathan Edwards*, 4.258.
20. *Works of Jonathan Edwards*, 4.260.
21. *Works of Jonathan Edwards*, 4.263.
22. *Works of Jonathan Edwards*, 4.267.
23. *Works of Jonathan Edwards*, 4.279.
24. *Works of Jonathan Edwards*, 4.281.
25. *Works of Jonathan Edwards*, 4.281-2.

MEETING WITH GOD - Robert Doyle

1. Peter Kaldor, *Who Goes Where? Who Doesn't Care?* (Sydney: Lancer, 1987), 16-18.
2. This is an estimate assuming that half of each congregation returned forms, and extrapolated from the 88 per cent of Anglican churches which participated. Although the diocese gave the total numbers of forms filled out, it gave no totals of the clerical head counts. However, working from the results of St Paul's Carlingford, of 903

attenders and 455 forms returned, that is about half, there were about 74,000 people in Anglican churches on that Sunday. This is approximately 1.9 per cent of Sydney's population, 7.6 per cent of Sydney's Anglican population.

3. Fiona Pfennigwerth, 'A Good New Prayer Book', *Australian Church Record* October 6, 1986, 8; 'To Wrap Up 1986', *Church Record* December 15, 1986, 5.